73 CRIME & DETECTION

74 RUSSIA

75 LIGHT

76 ENERGY

77 ELECTRICITY

78 FORCE & MOTION

79 CHEMISTRY

80 MATTER

81 TIME & SPACE

82 ASTRONOMY

83 EARTH

84 LIFE

85 EVOLUTION

86 ECOLOGY

87 HUMAN BODY

88 MEDICINE

89 TECHNOLOGY

90 ELECTRONICS

91 RENAISSANCE

92 IMPRESSIONISM

93 GOYA

94 MANET

95 MONET

96 VAN GOGH

97 WATERCOLOR

98 PERSPECTIVE

99 DANCE

100 FUTURE

101 MYTHOLOGY

102 LEONARDO & HIS TIMES

103 OLYMPICS

104 MEDIA & COMMUNICATION

105 TITANIC

106 FOOTBALL

107 HURRICANE & TORNADO

108 SOCCER

109 PRESIDENTS

110 BASEBALL

111 EPIDEMIC

112 WORLD WAR II

113 SUPER BOWL

114 CIVIL WAR

115 RESCUE

116 EVEREST

117 FIRST LADIES

118 WORLD WAR I

119 SHAKESPEARE

120 WILD WEST

121 AMERICAN REVOLUTION

122 INDIA

DORLING KINDERSLEY ᴰᴷ EYEWITNESS BOOKS

FUTURE

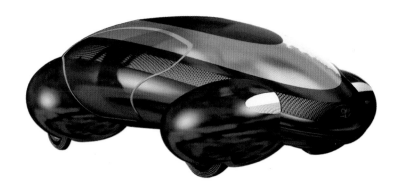

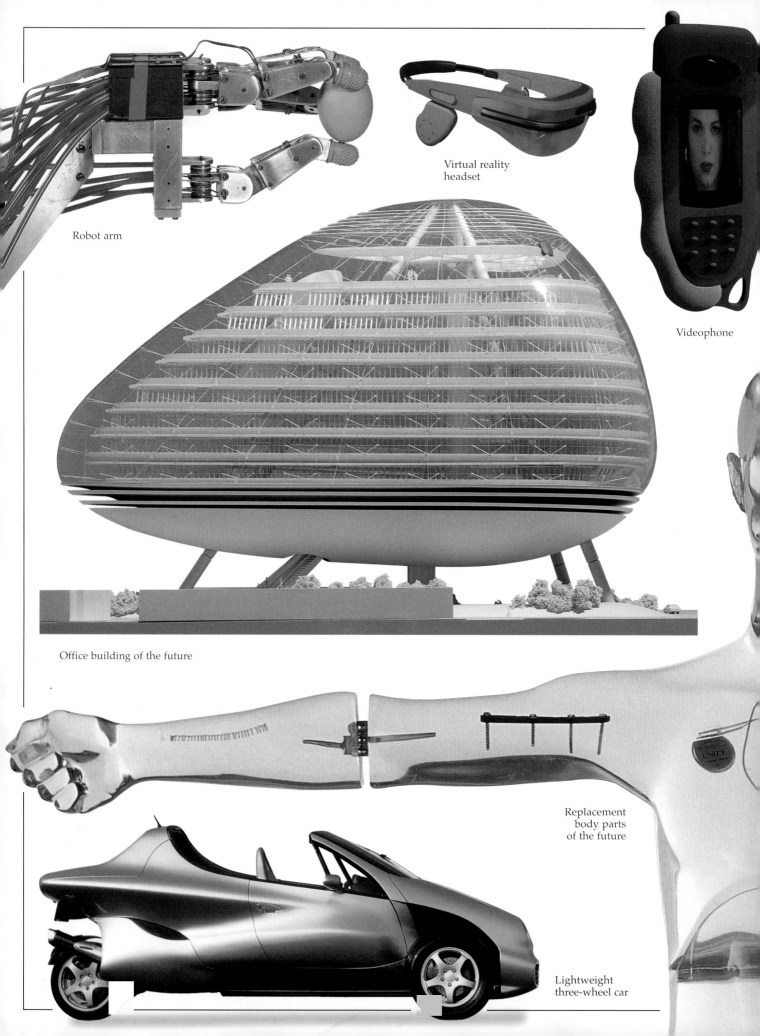

Robot arm

Virtual reality
headset

Videophone

Office building of the future

Replacement
body parts
of the future

Lightweight
three-wheel car

DK EYEWITNESS BOOKS

FUTURE

Written by
MICHAEL TAMBINI

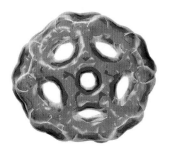

A buckyball

Dorling Kindersley

KAYSVILLE IUNIOR HIGH

Virtual reality robopal

Pocket-sized television

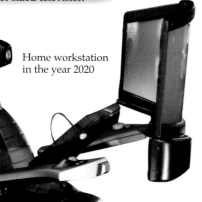

Home workstation
in the year 2020

Millennium
Tower, Tokyo

Dorling Kindersley
LONDON, NEW YORK, DELHI, JOHANNESBURG, MUNICH, PARIS and SYDNEY

For a full catalog, visit
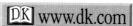 www.dk.com

Senior editor Miranda Smith
Editor Helena Spiteri
Senior art editor Jane Bull
Art editor Joanne Connor
Senior managing editor Linda Martin
Senior managing art editor Julia Harris
Production Lisa Moss
Picture research Sam Ruston
DTP Designer Nicky Studdart
Consultant Ian Pearson
Special photography Andy Crawford and David Exton

This Eyewitness ® Book has been conceived by
Dorling Kindersley Limited and Editions Gallimard

© 1998 Dorling Kindersley Limited
This edition © 2000 Dorling Kindersley Limited
First American edition, 1998

Published in the United States by
Dorling Kindersley Publishing, Inc.
375 Hudson Street,
New York, NY 10014
4 6 8 10 9 7 5 3

Library of Congress Cataloging-in-Publication Data
Tambini, Michael
Future / written by Michael Tambini.
p. cm. — (Eyewitness Books)
Includes index.
Summary: Provides a look ahead to the
technological, environmental, and biological
devlopments of the twenty-first century.
1. Technological forecasting—Juvenile literature.
[1. Technological forecasting. 2. Forecasting.]
I. Title
T174.T33 2000
601'.12—dc21
98–16440
ISBN 0-7894-5891-8 (pb)
ISBN 0-7894-5890-X (hc)

Color reproduction by Colourscan, Singapore
Printed in China by Toppan Printing Co. (Shenzhen) Ltd.

Contents

A brave new world

WE ARE FASCINATED by the future and excited by thinking about what might happen next. Through history, many people have tried to predict the future. Fortunetellers and prophets utter words of doom and warning, while futurologists anticipate scientific and social changes by analyzing existing trends. Imagine the 20th century without the car, telephone, computer, atom bomb, space travel, or the discovery of DNA. They have all made a profound impact on us – but which of them were predicted?

CRYSTAL-GAZING
For centuries, mystics and fortunetellers have made predictions. But their utterances owed more to a knowledge of human nature than anything else.

Different lines represent different characteristics

PALM READING
A popular form of prophecy is palm reading, which originated in India and has been practiced for hundreds of years. It is believed that a person's character and future can be discovered by the interpretation of the natural markings on his or her hands.

The Hand

Characters often signify future fates

IT'S IN THE CARDS
Cards are frequently used to predict the future. Before a reading can be made, the cards have to be shuffled, placed face down, then turned over one by one.

NOSTRADAMUS
The prophecies of Nostradamus were first published in the 16th century, and many believe he accurately foretold the future. He is said to have predicted the Great Fire of London and air battles in the 20th century.

SCIENCE FICTION
Science fiction writers are some of the most active forecasters of the future. Writers such as Jules Verne, H. G. Wells, Arthur C. Clarke, and Isaac Asimov have depicted worlds we may know well in the future.

DELPHIC ORACLE
In Greece, at the foot of Mount Parnassus, stood the temple of Apollo. Here Apollo spoke through his priestess, who predicted the future and gave guidance. Today, the closest we have to oracles are the futurologists who predict based on scientific information.

1900s

I never think of the future – it comes soon enough.

–ALBERT EINSTEIN

ALBERT EINSTE
In 1905, Einste proposed a theo of relativity, whi was to revolution the field of physi He later outlined complete theo of gravity th explained how t universe wor

TAKING PICTURES
Black-and-white photography became very popular at the turn of the century. But when the Lumière brothers developed color film in 1904, there was an even greater surge of interest in photography.

Pilot lay on his stomach

Pilot gently twists wings to control flight

TAKING FLIGHT
In 1903, the Wright brothers flew for just 12 seconds, covering a distance of 120 ft (37 m), an scarcely anyone paid attention. Yet this event changed the world. Today, we think nothing of traveling halfway around the world by jumbo je

INVENTIONS
1901 First transatlantic radio broadcast
1901 Hubert Cecil Booth manufactures the first vacuum cleaner
1903 Wright brothers make first powered fligh
1904 Lumière brothers develop color photography
1907 French bicycle maker Paul Cornu's moto driven helicopter takes to the air

EVENTS
1900 Sigmund Freud publishes his book Th *Interpretation of Dreams*
1902 Boer War ends in South Africa
1904 Japanese attack Port Arthur at start of Russo-Japanese War
1905 Albert Einstein proposes his theory of relativity
1908 Two-year-old Pu Yi ascends throne of Chi

1910s

Time present and time past are both perhaps present in time future, and time future contained in time past.

—T. S. ELIOT

MAKING CONTACT
The invention of the telephone began the great communications revolution. For the first time, it was possible to talk directly to people over great distances.

METAL THAT LASTS
By adding chromium to steel in 1913, a new metal that would not rust or scratch was created. Stainless steel has become a common part of everyday life.

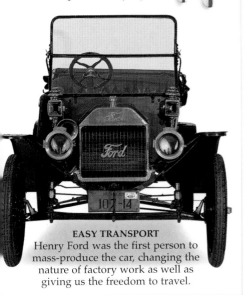

EASY TRANSPORT
Henry Ford was the first person to mass-produce the car, changing the nature of factory work as well as giving us the freedom to travel.

1913 Mass production of Ford's Model T begins
1913 Stainless steel first cast in Sheffield, England
1914 First traffic lights introduced in Ohio
1915 Heat-resistant glass Pyrex marketed
1915 First transcontinental telephone call between New York and San Francisco
1916 First tank goes into battle

1911 Norwegian Roald Amundsen reaches the South Pole
1911 Revolution in China overthrows the Ch'ing dynasty
1912 *Titanic* sinks in the Atlantic
1914 Start of World War I, which ends with German surrender in 1918
1917 Tsar Nicholas II overthrown in Russia

1920s

The most distressing thing that can happen to a prophet is to be proved wrong. The next most distressing thing is to be proved right.

—ALDOUS HUXLEY

A SCREEN IN THE LIVING ROOM
For more than half a century, television has provided us with news, drama, and entertainment. Viewers in the home have been eyewitnesses to historic events, from civil wars to the death of a president.

WALL STREET CRASH
The Wall Street stock market crash in 1929 led to financial crisis across the world. In the United States, farming businesses collapsed, unemployment rose, and banks failed.

1920 "Tommy" submachine gun patented
1921 18 million Russians starve because of severe drought
1921 First highway opens in Germany
1922 First diabetic treated with insulin, Canada
1925 John Logie Baird transmits first television pictures

1920 Prohibition comes into force
1922 Tutankhamun's tomb uncovered, Egypt
1928 Flying doctor service begins in Australia
1928 Scottish bacteriologist Alexander Fleming discovers penicillin
1929 Wall Street crash leads to world financial crisis

1930s

You cannot fight against the future. Time is on our side.

—WILLIAM GLADSTONE

Nylon stockings

NYLON
Few materials have had such an impact on the fashion industry as nylon. This manufactured material was used to make many different products.

Whittle's jet engine

JET ENGINE
In 1937, British engineer Frank Whittle built the first prototype of a jet engine, which was put to practical use in 1941. Today, jet aircraft can travel faster than the speed of sound.

WRITING OF THE FUTURE
H. G. Wells wrote many science fiction novels, including *The War of the Worlds*, in which the Earth is invaded.

Wells at work on a novel

1933 German post office opens the first "telex" service between Berlin and Hamburg
1934 British inventor Percy Shaw patents cat's-eye road studs
1935 Nylon developed by Wallace Carothers
1935 Kodak introduces the first color film
1937 Engineer Frank Whittle builds prototype of the first jet engine

1930 Clyde Tombaugh discovers Pluto
1936 Spanish Civil War begins
1937 Airship *Hindenburg* bursts into flames, killing 35 of the 97 on board
1938 Orson Welles broadcasts convincing radio version of H. G. Wells's *The War of the Worlds*
1939 Germany, under Adolf Hitler, invades Poland and starts World War II

Continued on next page

1940s

We have to live with the bugs and the bomb not for the next ten years but the next ten thousand.

–ARTHUR KOESTLER

Distinctive mushroom cloud

ATOM BOMB
The atom bombs that destroyed Hiroshima and Nagasaki in 1945 left few doubts about their awesome potential, and so began an arms race among world powers.

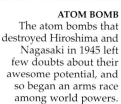

ARTHUR C. CLARKE
Arthur C. Clarke has written many science fiction novels about space exploration. He also predicted the use of satellites for global communications.

1950s

We are going to have to be rather clever to escape from our own cleverness in the past.

–SIR MARK OLIPHANT

DINERS' CLUB
The Diners' Club card was set up to make it easier for executives to eat out on a company account. Now credit cards are used everywhere and may soon replace cash.

SILICON CHIP
The impact of silicon chips on this century cannot be overstated. Tiny wafers of silicon carry thousands of electrical components and are used everywhere, from computers to cars.

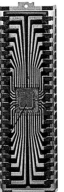

Silicon chip

FRANCIS CRICK AND JAMES WATSON
In 1953, Frances Crick and James Watson discovered the molecular structure of DNA. The genetic code for all life is contained within this molecule. Our ability to understand and manipulate it will be central to the 21st century.

CREDIT
IDENTIFICATION
CARD
the Diners' Club
SIGNATURE
EXPIRES JUNE 30, 1951
SUBJECT TO TERMS OF REVERSE SIDE

1960s

TELSTAR
Telstar was the first communications satellite to orbit the Earth. It was owned by AT&T and launched by NASA.

Th future called perhaps which is th only possibl thing to call i And the mos importan thing is no to allow it t scare you

–TENNESSEE WILLIA

MAN ON THE MOO
As Neil Armstron stepped onto the moon, he uttered now historic wor "That's one sma step for a man, one giant leap mankind." Th exploration space is stil in its infanc yet human seem drive to explore, a people are certain to follow in Neil Armstrong's footste

Neil Armstro on the surfac of the moon

INVENTIONS		
1941 World's first aerosol can patented 1943 Dutch doctor Wilhelm Kolff makes first artificial kidney machine 1945 Arthur C. Clarke predicts satellites in geostationary orbit for global communications 1945 Microwave oven patented 1947 First transistor made 1949 Maiden flight of the Comet jet	1950 First credit card, Diners' Club, introduced 1951 Engineers John Eckert and John Mauchly invent digital computer UNIVAC 1957 USSR launches *Sputnik 1*, first artificial satellite in space 1959 British designer Christopher Cockerell invents the hovercraft 1959 First silicon chip manufactured	1960 Theodore Maiman builds the laser 1962 First communications satellite, *Telstar I*, put into orbit 1963 Tape cassette machine patented by Phillips, Holland 1966 Vertical take-off and landing (VTOL) aircraft unveiled at air show 1967 France launches its first nuclear submarine

EVENTS		
1945 World War II ends with Hitler's suicide 1945 Atom bombs dropped on Hiroshima and Nagasaki 1947 Pilot Chuck Yeager breaks the sound barrier 1948 South Africa's Nationalist party comes to power and imposes apartheid 1949 NATO formed	1950 North Korea invades South Korea 1953 Francis Crick and James Watson discover the structure of DNA 1953 Edmund Hillary of New Zealand and Tenzing Norgay of Nepal climb Mt. Everest 1954 British athlete Roger Bannister runs a mile in under four minutes 1955 Disneyland opens in California	1961 Cosmonaut Yuri Gagarin becomes the firs man in space 1961 East German wall divides the city of Berli 1963 President John F. Kennedy assassinated 1967 Six-Day War in Israel 1967 Christiaan Barnard performs first heart transplant in South Africa 1969 First man lands on the moon

1970s

We should all be concerned about the future because we will have to spend the rest of our lives there.

–C. F. KETTERING

FLOPPY DISK
Computer users in the 1970s were able to record data and install programs using disks that were literally floppy. Information is now often stored on compact discs (CDs).

BAR CODE
Information stored on a computer can be quickly accessed using a bar code. Bar codes have revolutionized supermarket checkouts, where the scanner reads the product labels.

CONCORDE
Since 1976, *Concorde* – a joint project by British Airways and French Airways – has flown at supersonic speeds across the Atlantic. It is criticized for causing noise pollution.

Concorde

1980s

Science fiction is a kind of archaeology of the future.

–CLIFTON FADIMAN

SPACE SHUTTLE
The space shuttle is the first reusable manned spacecraft. The first four space shuttles were named after famous ships, *Columbia, Challenger, Endeavour,* and *Atlantis,* reminding us how much humankind loves to explore.

Antenna

MOBILE PHONE
Our ability to make immediate contact with each other regardless of where we are is now taken for granted. Lightweight mobile telephones are becoming as familiar as wristwatches. Portable computers linked to telephones will allow access to the Internet in the future.

1990s

Such abundance of fire and fiery missiles shall fall from the heavens that nothing shall escape the holocaust. And this will occur before the last conflagration – in 1999.

–NOSTRADAMUS

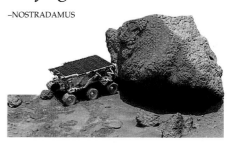

DESTINATION MARS
The *Pathfinder* probe landed on Mars on July 4, 1997. It released the Sojourner, a wheeled vehicle, which explored the Martian landscape. NASA is now making preparations to send the first astronauts to the red planet.

Headset gives 3-D vision

Data glove

VIRTUAL REALITY
Virtual reality is already being used for entertainment, as well as for medicine and design. In the future, virtual reality will become as familiar to us as movies.

1970 IBM creates the first floppy disk
1971 Food processor invented in France
1971 Soviet Union puts space station into orbit
1972 CT scanner introduced by British researcher Godfrey Hounsfield
1976 Supersonic airliner *Concorde* makes first commercial flight
1979 Catalytic converter developed in Britain

1981 World's first space shuttle, *Columbia,* blasts off
1981 Stealth fighter plane has maiden flight in America
1982 First artificial heart implanted
1984 Genetic fingerprinting introduced
1985 Desktop (DTP) publishing created
1985 Mobile phones launched in Europe

1990 Sony produces Data Discman, an electronic book
1991 *ERS-1,* Europe's first environmental satellite, goes into orbit
1992 Virtual reality is developed as a 3-D video game in America
1993 First voice-operated TV/radio remote control is launched

---

1973 Australia's Sydney Opera House completed amid controversy
1973 Last American troops leave Vietnam, but war does not end for two years
1973 Bar codes first introduced on products for sale in America
1979 Nuclear accident at Three Mile Island, Pennsylvania

1980 Mt. St. Helens erupts in Washington
1982 Argentine forces surrender Falkland Islands to Britain
1985 Live Aid concert watched by 1.5 million people
1986 Space shuttle *Challenger* explodes
1986 Major nuclear accident at Chernobyl
1989 Berlin wall torn down

1990 Saddam Hussein of Iraq invades Kuwait
1992 Civil war breaks out in Yugoslavia
1992 Hole in ozone layer stretches over the coast of South America for the first time
1994 ANC leader Nelson Mandela elected as first black president of South Africa
1997 "Mad cow disease" leads to ban on British beef imports

A shrinking planet

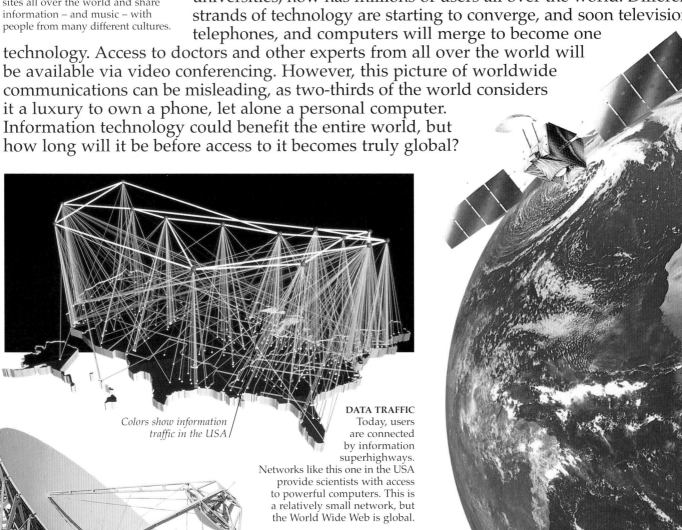

THE WORLD IS GETTING SMALLER, or so it seems. Today, there are 150 communications satellites in geostationary orbit around the Earth, gathering information and enabling us to communicate with each other. Mobile phones, fax machines, and electronic mail keep us in touch wherever we are. Instant news reports, from cultural events to wars and famine, are routinely transmitted into our homes. The Internet, which began as a modest communications network between a number of universities, now has millions of users all over the world. Different strands of technology are starting to converge, and soon televisions, telephones, and computers will merge to become one technology. Access to doctors and other experts from all over the world will be available via video conferencing. However, this picture of worldwide communications can be misleading, as two-thirds of the world considers it a luxury to own a phone, let alone a personal computer. Information technology could benefit the entire world, but how long will it be before access to it becomes truly global?

GETTING WIRED
Technology has certainly come a long way since this group gathered to listen to the latest sound recording! Via the Internet, it is now possible to connect to sites all over the world and share information – and music – with people from many different cultures.

Colors show information traffic in the USA

DATA TRAFFIC
Today, users are connected by information superhighways. Networks like this one in the USA provide scientists with access to powerful computers. This is a relatively small network, but the World Wide Web is global.

SENDING AND RECEIVING MESSAGES
The first satellite, *Sputnik 1,* was launched in 1957. Since then over two thousand more satellites have been sent into space, although only a fraction of them are operating today. On the ground all around the world, satellite dishes (left) transmit and receive news and information. Many different countries have put into orbit geostationary communications satellites such as the *Intelsat K* (above right), and television satellites such as the *TDF-1* (right).

day's
deophones are
aller and less
lky than this

E MORE OF YOUR FRIENDS
his comical image from a 1956 magazine
ustrates how people believed that having a
deophone would invade privacy. It was not
til the 1990s that technological advances
ade these machines a practical possibility.

FACE TO FACE
Video conferencing is already a
popular form of communication
among international businesses
because it saves the time and
expense of travel. Business people
can hold meetings face-to-face,
even though they may live and
work at opposite ends of the globe. The system is also
being used in schools, where experts from all over the
world can be invited into the classroom to lecture
or teach via video conferencing.

Equipment allows doctor to
be "virtually present"
at scene of accident

A panel of solar cells
collects and stores
energy until someone
wants to make a call

Headset is fitted
with video camera,
television screen,
and microphone

Doctor views
images sent from
paramedic's
camera and gives
medical advice

SAVING LIVES
It will not be long before a paramedic
at the scene of an accident will be able
to receive on-the-spot advice from a
doctor at a hospital. The paramedic
will receive diagrams showing him
or her what to do. This life-saving
equipment is a combination of video
conferencing software and a satellite
communications network.

SOLAR TELEPHONES
Many places around
the world have
no electricity. Solar
power may provide
the answer. This
solar-powered
telephone booth
uses the sun to
generate energy to
transmit and
receive calls.

FIBER OPTICS
Flexible, threadlike
strands of the purest
glass have replaced
copper wire in the cables
used to transmit telephone
and television signals.
They can carry much
more information and
are specially treated so
transmissions pass through
them with minimum distortion.
This means high volumes of
images or telephone conversations
can be carried. There are now
hundreds of thousands of miles
of fiber optic cables around the world.

A fiber the same
thickness as a human
hair can carry about
one million
conversations
simultaneously

Watching the Earth

1 THE BLUE PLANET
In the 1960s, satellites and astronauts sent back the first pictures of our planet from space. From a long distance, our planet is predominantly blue and, compared with the giant scale of the universe, looks small and fragile.

HAVE YOU EVER WONDERED what your house looks like from space? Well, soon you will be able to find out. Satellite imaging is becoming so sophisticated that it is now possible to see every square yard of Earth from deep in space. One day in the future, not only will you be able to see your own house from space, you will even be able to read a newspaper left out on the lawn. The author George Orwell (1903-50) predicted a future in which our every move would be monitored by governments obsessed with control. In some ways he was right. Today, satellites watch us from space, and video cameras record our movements in shopping centers and other public places. But satellites have a variety of other useful purposes. Views of the Earth from the *Landsat* satellite provide us with vital ecological information. Satellites can also inform us of changes in urban and environmental conditions, and warn us in advance of any major ecological problem threatening the Earth.

BIG BROTHER IS WATCHING YOU
George Orwell's gloomy novel of the future, *1984*, predicted a society dominated by state control. Video screens not only provided constant propaganda but were also linked to surveillance cameras. Terrified citizens were rarely out of the sight of "Big Brother."

2 CLOUDLESS SKIES OVER EUROPE
With today's technology, satellites out in space can pinpoint particular details on Earth, such as expanses of vegetation, large rivers, deserts, and huge mountain ranges. But in order to do this, it is essential that the satellite's view is not obscured by thick layers of clouds. This sequence has been put together with cloudless images taken by a satellite.

Cloudless image of Italy

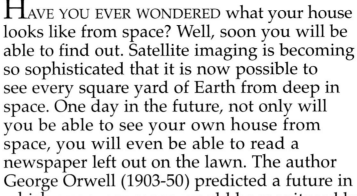

3 MOVING CLOSER
Zooming in even closer, it is possible to see additional detail. In the north of Italy, the southern Alps mountain range comes into focus. The pictures have been produced by taking thousands of satellite images and piecing them together with a computer. Using cameras that are able to home in to provide close detail, it is possible to see a small area of a continent.

Eye of the storm at the heart of the hurricane

WATCHING THE WEATHER
Satellites and spacecraft allow meteorologists to monitor weather conditions on Earth. This view from the space shuttle *Atlantis* shows Hurricane Florence in 1988 as it swept dangerously across the Atlantic Ocean. Weather satellites in orbit can see how clouds are moving, and forecasters use this information to predict the weather.

Southern Alps mountain range

4 MOUNTAIN SCENERY
The snowcapped ridges of the mountain range come into view. So far, this photographic technique has been used only by the militaries of various countries, but will soon be available for commercial purposes. It will be possible to own pictures of your house taken from space.

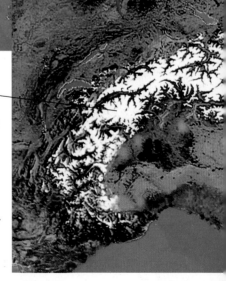

View of the city center of Washington, D.C.

E IN THE SKY
e first *Landsat* satellite was
unched in 1974 to monitor
anges on Earth. Since then, four
ccessors have been launched, each
oviding increasingly detailed data
out urban areas, deforestation,
llution, and natural disasters.

Highest ozone concentration

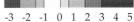

TEMPERATURE TRENDS
These computer-generated maps
show world temperature trends. The
evidence suggests that temperatures
will increase considerably in the 21st
century, which many believe to be
an indication of global warming. If
this is the case, the consequences
will be devastating for many
parts of the world.

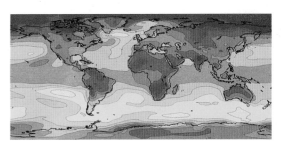

Predicted temperatures for 2050

-1 0 1 2 3 4 5

OZONE DEPLETION
The ozone layer shields
Earth from the Sun's
harmful ultraviolet
rays, but certain
gases are depleting
the protective layer.
This picture (left)
shows the ozone hole
over Antarctica. The
colors show ozone
concentration, from
dark red for the lowest
to green for the highest.

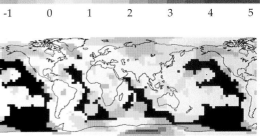

Temperature trends 1965-1985

-3 -2 -1 0 1 2 3 4 5

5 IN DETAIL
It is now possible to see clearly the details of
the thick vegetation in the valleys between the high
mountains in the range. At this distance, we can
make out the courses the rivers follow and how
much snow covers the giant mountaintops.

Contours of the rivers

6 HOMING IN
Satellite imaging is able to
focus on a 3-ft (1-m) area. So, from
space it is possible to take pictures
of a rock on the face of the
Matterhorn. In the future,
imaging systems may even
take us underground or
allow us to explore
the deepest depths
of the oceans.

3-D image of Matterhorn

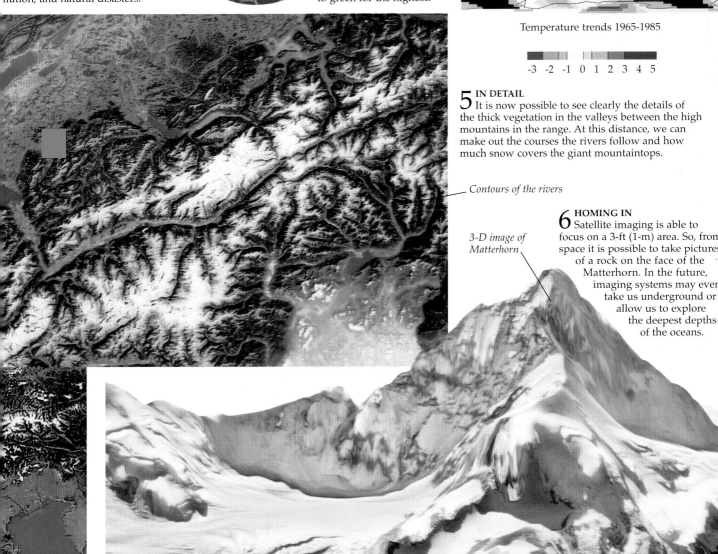

The growing world

THE WORLD'S POPULATION IS GROWING at an incredible rate. In the last 200 years it has accelerated from about one billion to over six billion, and is now only beginning to show signs of slowing down. The birth rate is higher than the death rate and, according to the social scientists who study population trends, these rates are unlikely to balance out until the world population reaches 10 or 11 billion. With advanced medical care, improved living conditions, and a healthier diet in the future, we will live longer, be more active, and have a better quality of life. But if the planet is to sustain such a high population, it will be necessary to preserve and protect its natural resources. Nations will have to work together to reduce pollution, protect the forests, control pesticides, and find alternative sources of energy to fossil fuels.

TOO MANY MOUTHS TO FEED
Overpopulation puts a strain on resources. In many countries, a natural disaster, such as flooding or crop failure, already causes famine. The lack of clean drinking water or an inadequate supply of food will devastate entire communities.

GETTING OLDER
Improved medical care, a better diet, and a healthier lifestyle lead not only to a longer life but also to a fitter one. Because of this, it is likely that, many people will live to the age of 100 or more from the beginning of the 21st century.

Population in billion

GROWING POPULATION
In just over a century, the world's population has tripled in size. Up until the early 1800s, the population remained under one billion. However, better health and living conditions resulted in the birth rate exceeding the death rate, and by 1900, there were two billion people in the world. Less than 50 years later, the population reached three billion. Today, it has reached more than six billion, and is expected to continue to rise at a rate of about one billion every 12 years. This chart shows the dramatic rise in billions from 1800, showing how the numbers are likely to become stable from 2100 onwards.

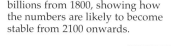

| 1800 | 1850 | 1900 | 1950 | 2000 | 2050 | 2100 | 2150 | Year |

CITY SPRAWL
The world's population is concentrating more and more in urban areas. Cities with a million inhabitants are commonplace, and some exceed this – the metropolitan area of Tokyo, Japan, already has a population of over 29 million. Today, 37 percent of the population of developing countries lives in cities, and this figure is expected to rise, increasing the pressure to provide jobs, housing, and public services.

POLLUTED ATMOSPHERES
We consume billions of tonnes of fossil fuels every year, using up natural resources and polluting the atmosphere. The exhaust fumes from motor vehicles, together with emissions from factories, produce noxious smogs that have catastrophic consequences both for people's health and for the environment.

Power station in Moscow

THIRST FOR FOREIGN CULTURE
Certain cultures have become more attractive and desirable than others. The American way of life has a huge impact on the desire for consumer goods throughout the world. In the future, such a demand for consumer goods may deplete our natural resources.

Coca-Cola is successfully exported throughout the world

More than 668 million drinks of Coca-Cola are consumed worldwide every day

Slum dwellings lie not far from modern buildings in Sao Paulo, Brazil

CONSERVING OUR FUTURE
The high demand for timber and agricultural land has meant that vast tracts of South American jungle are being lost forever. This has a devastating effect on plants and animals, and causes enormous damage to the Earth's atmosphere. Governments must promote better agricultural practices before it is too late.

GROWTH OF DEVELOPING COUNTRIES
When poor agricultural workers migrate from the countryside to urban areas they put a great strain on the work market, housing, and public services – the city's infrastructure. Around 37 percent of the population of developing countries live in cities, and this figure is expected to rise to 50 percent in the next few years.

Environmentally friendly

TECHNOLOGICAL PROGRESS HAS provided us with many advantages, and will continue to do so in the future, but not without a price – the damaged ozone layer and the effects of greenhouse gases may have terrible consequences for the future of our planet. Air pollution is causing acid rain, and water contamination is killing wildlife. Natural resources are rapidly being used up, and many large tracts of rain forest have been destroyed. Because of our actions, some of the animals on our planet have become extinct, while others are endangered. If we do not take a more responsible attitude toward our finite resources, the results will be catastrophic.

VISIONS OF THE FUTURE
Creating your own artificially controlled environment once seemed an exciting prospect. Some architects have taken great pleasure in designing future homes, such as this one, from the 1950s, which rotates to face any direction. A climate-conditioned dome makes it possible to enjoy summer activities in the middle of winter. Such schemes can be seen today in vacation resorts and leisure centers.

IDEAL FOR THE CITY OF THE FUTURE
The car is a very popular form of transportation. But people are concerned by the levels of pollution it produces and the future scarcity of gas. Manufacturers are therefore designing cars with clean, fuel-efficient engines.

ALTERNATIVE TO GAS
Scientists around the world are searching for alternatives to non-renewable and expensive fossil fuels. Alcohol, which is made from distilled grain, is one alternative to gas. It has been successfully used as fuel in countries without natural oil reserves.

Lightweight body means engine has to do less work and so requires less fuel

Honda's solar car in the World Solar Challenge Race

POWERED BY THE SUN
A solar-powered vehicle uses solar cells to convert energy from the sun into electricity, which drives its electric motors. But solar cars are still little more than expensive novelties and fall short of the performance required by many motorists.

SOLAR POWER STATION
Solar energy has enormous potential, but it is costly to collect and difficult to convert and store. Flat-plate collectors are used in some homes for heating water, but because of the relatively low temperatures produced, it is not practical to convert the heat energy into electricity. Concentrating collectors (left) can focus sunlight onto a single point and generate temperatures high enough to power steam-turbine electric generators. A computer turns the dishes to make sure they face the sun throughout the day.

Streamlined shape allows wind to flow smoothly

Building supported by tripod megastructure

reasingly, people are
coming aware of the
lue of recycling. Today,
 generate an enormous
ount of waste, and
ere are increasing
oblems with its
posal. In the future,
 will manufacture
oducts that are built to
t and can be repaired.
ey will be easily
mantled and reused
sometimes surprising
ys (right) or at least
posed of safely
d efficiently.

Rubber tire is
removed from car

Tire ready to be re-formed
after shredding

Handbag made from
shredded car tire

t, stale air is vented
ough louver at the
of the building

In winter, warm air at the
top is used to heat cold air
coming in at the bottom

Air between glass
skins is heated by
solar radiation

Mirrors reflect
natural light into
offices

OFFICE OF THE FUTURE

Most traditional offices are not environmentally friendly.
They consume high levels of energy in winter, and require
even more to keep them cool in summer. They often lack a
natural source of air and light, and so keep electric lighting
and air conditioning switched on all day. This not only
results in high fuel costs but is also unpleasant for the
occupants. As the cost of fuels rises, energy-
inefficient office buildings will need to be
redesigned. This remarkable-looking
office building has been designed to
address exactly these problems by
maximizing the use of both
natural ventilation and light.

Air conditioning is
replaced by a natural
ventilation system

Building stands high
above ground, away
from pollution

Continued from previous page

Insulated box inside a glass house

Home of the future

Most houses built today take advantage of energy-saving features, but few are as well-designed as the Integer Millennium House in England. This high-tech building dramatically reduces the consumption of natural resources. It is designed as a house within a house – an inner box surrounded by a glass house. The lower floor is below ground level, sheltered by earth on three sides. The upper levels are made from lightweight materials for easy and fast construction. Mowing the lawn will present a new challenge, as the most unusual feature of the house is the roof, which is covered with grass.

Lightweight house built on solid foundation

Lower part of house sheltered by earth on three sides

Corrugated layer under grass stores water for roof while keeping it out the house

Prefabricated partitions installed as needed

Walls are made from cement and covered with tiles

RECYCLING THE EASY W

Recycling waste in this house will not be a cho
There are waste separation bins in their own are
Outside, rainwater is collected in a pool and c
be used to water the garden or wash the car. The
are also compost bins to recycle organic was

Glass house provides a controlled climate

Even the shed has a grass roof

CENTRAL SERVICES

A central core gives easy access to the plumbing and electrical services. Electricity and communications lines are run through this core into the house by cable. This means that it is easy to make any repairs. A telephone-operated computer controls the energy-efficient lighting, appliances, and heating installations. The computer also controls a smoke and fire detector and the security systems that protect the house.

Central core gives direct access to service controls

Plants can be grown inside glass house

Pool for storing rainwater

Compost bin organic waste

FLEXIBLE HOUSE

The inside of the house can be adjusted according to the needs of the occupants. The bathroom and kitchen are prefabricated and attached to the central services core, but the rest of the space is adaptable. The general structure is open, and partitions can divide the house, allowing the owners to change the number of rooms as needed.

Energy-efficient internal lighting can be pre-programmed

Dishwasher and stove can be controlled remotely

Heating is under the floor rather than in the wall, which makes it easy to move partitions

Prefabricated kitche connects to the central core

Partition walls can be moved to make extra rooms where necessary

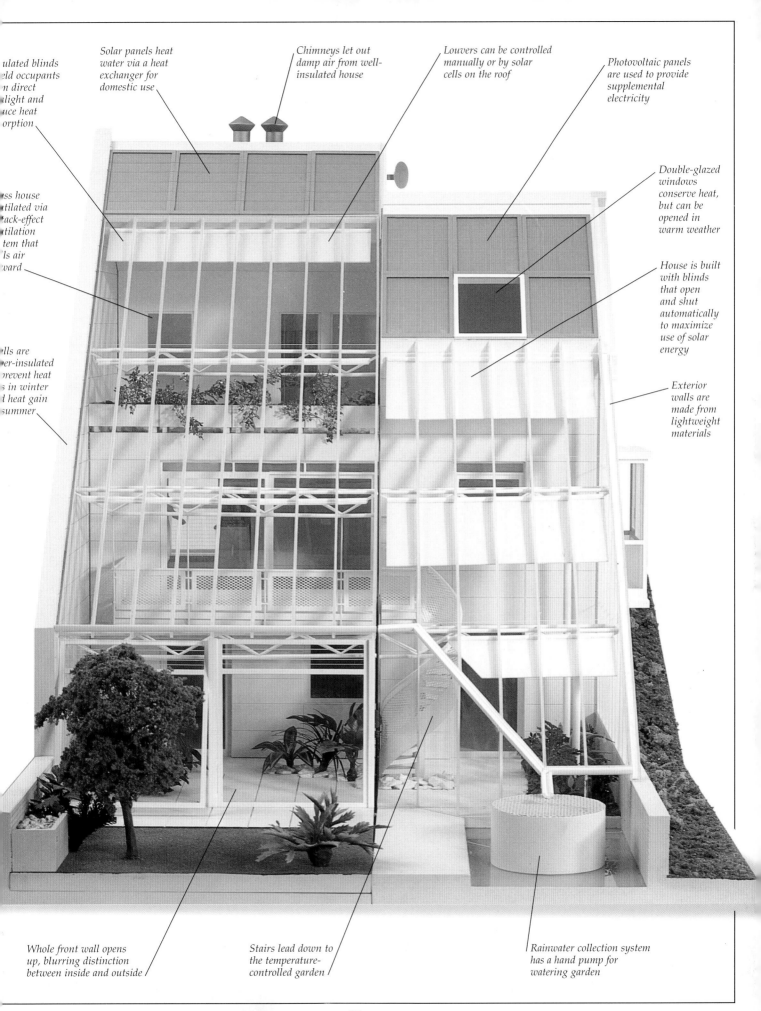

ulated blinds
eld occupants
n direct
light and
uce heat
orption

Solar panels heat
water via a heat
exchanger for
domestic use

Chimneys let out
damp air from well-
insulated house

Louvers can be controlled
manually or by solar
cells on the roof

Photovoltaic panels
are used to provide
supplemental
electricity

ss house
tilated via
ack-effect
tilation
tem that
ls air
ward

Double-glazed
windows
conserve heat,
but can be
opened in
warm weather

House is built
with blinds
that open
and shut
automatically
to maximize
use of solar
energy

lls are
er-insulated
prevent heat
s in winter
d heat gain
summer

Exterior
walls are
made from
lightweight
materials

Whole front wall opens
up, blurring distinction
between inside and outside

Stairs lead down to
the temperature-
controlled garden

Rainwater collection system
has a hand pump for
watering garden

Futuropolis

PEOPLE HAVE TRADITIONALLY BEEN ATTRACTED to living in cities because of the cultural and economic opportunities they offer. It will not be long before most people become urban dwellers. It will be necessary to build new cities and rebuild existing cities to accommodate the huge increase in the world's population. These cities will need to be planned very carefully, and existing transportation systems will have to be redesigned. High-rise offices and apartment towers, taller than ever before, will become self-contained, with their own shops, restaurants, and leisure facilities. They will operate like small towns, and the occupants will rarely need to leave them. The pollution caused by increased numbers of people will need to be managed, so the internal combustion engine will be banned and buildings will be energy-efficient, making use of renewable energy.

CITY-BUILDING FOR THE NEW MILLENNIUM

One answer to potential overcrowding is to build upward, constructing huge structures like the proposed Millennium Tower, to be built in Daiba Bay, Tokyo, Japan, in the early 21st century. The tower will be a self-contained township 150 stories high, with a population of 50,000. High-speed double-decker elevators will carry 80 people at a time to "sky centers," where they can visit restaurants and shops, or enjoy all forms of entertainment, including the cinema or discos. From the sky centers, residents will travel by conventional high-speed elevators to their apartments or places of work on the other floors.

Towers can withstand high winds and earthquakes

2,755 ft (840 m)

1,483 ft (451.9 m)

1,250 ft (381 m)

Millennium Tower

Petronas Towers

Empire State

FLYING CITIES

This is how one visionary of 1929 saw New York in the future – as a traveling city suspended high above the ground. The nearest we are likely to come to cities in the sky are spaceships that will orbit the Earth.

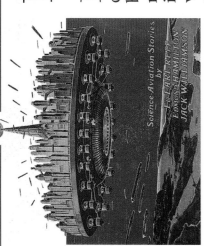

Science Aviation Stories by EARL REPP, EDMOND HAMILTON, JACK WILLIAMSON

Empire State Building

BUILDING HIGH

Today's Manhattan skyline demonstrates one architectural solution to the lack of space. Some of the world's tallest buildings are among those that crowd the island city of New York. The high price of land in the city encouraged architects to construct tall steel-framed skyscrapers on small lots.

HOTELS OF THE FUTURE

Huge numbers of Japanese commuters often stay in Tokyo's extraordinary space-saving hotels overnight. Each individual sleeps in a capsule that is air-conditioned and

Honeycomb hotel rooms in Tokyo, Japan

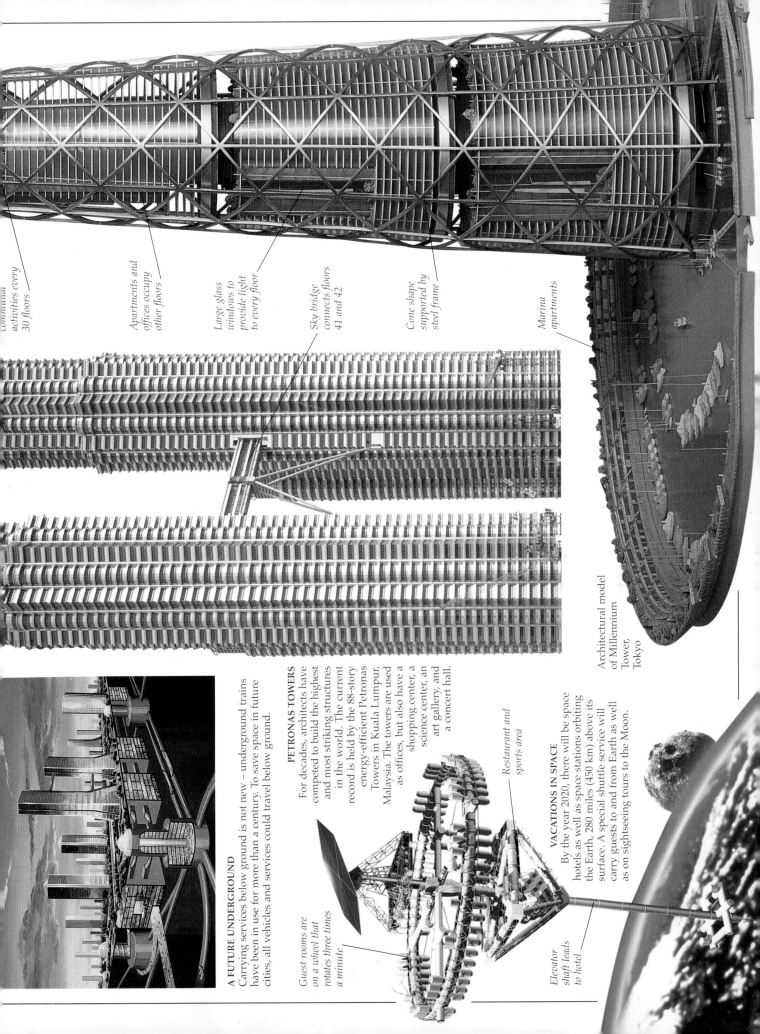

Communal activities every 30 floors

Apartments and offices occupy other floors

Large glass windows to provide light to every floor

Sky bridge connects floors 41 and 42

Cone shape supported by steel frame

Marina apartments

Architectural model of Millennium Tower, Tokyo

A FUTURE UNDERGROUND

Carrying services below ground is not new – underground trains have been in use for more than a century. To save space in future cities, all vehicles and services could travel below ground.

Guest rooms are on a wheel that rotates three times a minute

PETRONAS TOWERS

For decades, architects have competed to build the highest and most striking structures in the world. The current record is held by the 88-story energy-efficient Petronas Towers in Kuala Lumpur, Malaysia. The towers are used as offices, but also have a shopping center, a science center, an art gallery, and a concert hall.

Restaurant and sports area

VACATIONS IN SPACE

By the year 2020, there will be space hotels as well as space stations orbiting the Earth, 280 miles (450 km) above its surface. A special shuttle service will carry guests to and from Earth as well as on sightseeing tours to the Moon.

Elevator shaft leads to hotel

Traffic control

THE FREEDOM TO TRAVEL IS VALUED highly, yet it is essential that we reduce fuel consumption, control pollution, and manage our busy roads. In the future, journeys will be planned in advance for optimum efficiency. By displaying position data on a digital map, a satellite-linked navigation system will ensure that drivers know their exact location. They will simply indicate their desired destination, and the car will provide detailed instructions on the best way to get there. A powerful onboard computer will monitor the car's movements, and will take action, such as turning off the engine if erratic driving indicates that the driver is about to fall asleep. On long-distance journeys, it will be possible to drive on an automated highway where the car will travel in a convoy, its speed and steering controlled by the computer. In the air, improved tracking systems will mean that more aircraft can travel safely without crowding or collisions. The Future Air Navigational System (FANS) will allow pilots to switch routes to take advantage of jet streams, which will speed up travel across the world as well as saving on fuel.

ACCURATE PREDICTION
As early as 1919, it was already obvious that the number of cars in densely populated cities was going to cause parking problems. The suggested solution, a multi-story parking garage, is now a familiar sight. Unfortunately, building more garages may only encourage more people to drive.

Car is powered by electricity

ELECTRICAL HIGHWAY
This advertisement from the 1950s suggests a future free of accidents and traffic jams. The car is propelled along an electrical superhighway, its speed and steering controlled by electronic devices embedded in the road. The family just sits back, playing board games and enjoying the journey.

AUTOMATED HIGHWAY
Today the automated highway is becoming a reality. Experiments are taking place with cars that can steer, accelerate, and brake by themselves. They are fitted with computers that pick up signals from magnets set in the road. They are designed to travel in convoys along designated stretches of highways.

Using this computer simulation, researchers can predict the behavior of drivers under different conditions

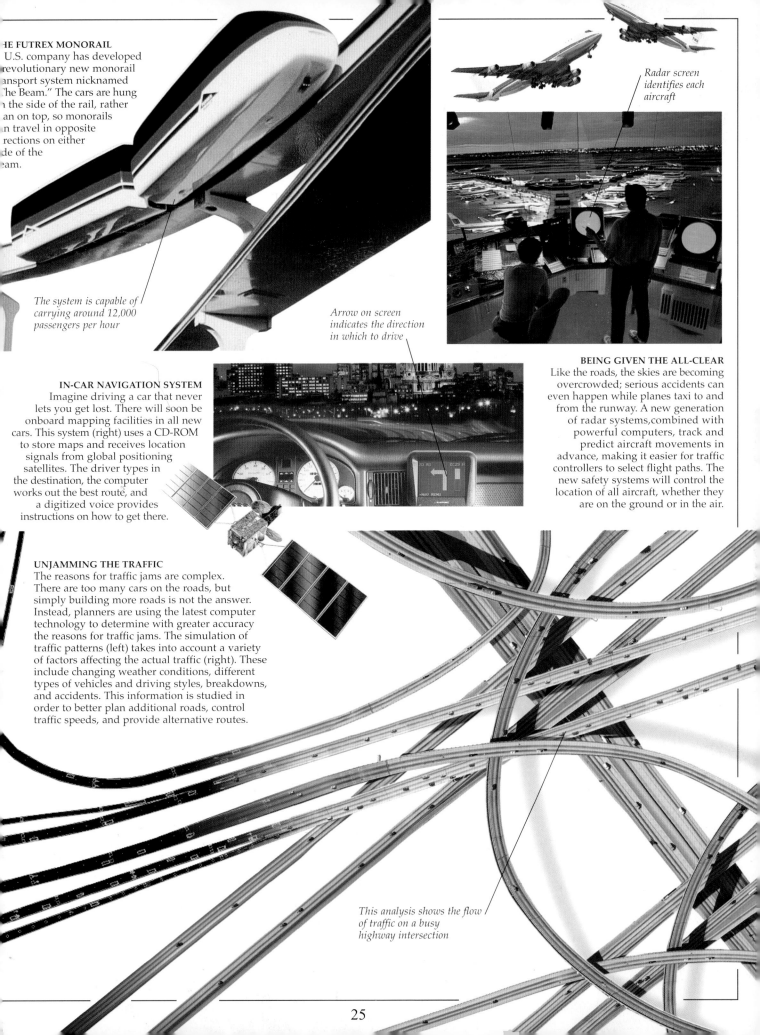

THE FUTREX MONORAIL
[A] U.S. company has developed [a] revolutionary new monorail [tr]ansport system nicknamed ["T]he Beam." The cars are hung [o]n the side of the rail, rather [th]an on top, so monorails [ca]n travel in opposite [di]rections on either [si]de of the [be]am.

The system is capable of carrying around 12,000 passengers per hour

Radar screen identifies each aircraft

Arrow on screen indicates the direction in which to drive

IN-CAR NAVIGATION SYSTEM
Imagine driving a car that never lets you get lost. There will soon be onboard mapping facilities in all new cars. This system (right) uses a CD-ROM to store maps and receives location signals from global positioning satellites. The driver types in the destination, the computer works out the best route, and a digitized voice provides instructions on how to get there.

BEING GIVEN THE ALL-CLEAR
Like the roads, the skies are becoming overcrowded; serious accidents can even happen while planes taxi to and from the runway. A new generation of radar systems, combined with powerful computers, track and predict aircraft movements in advance, making it easier for traffic controllers to select flight paths. The new safety systems will control the location of all aircraft, whether they are on the ground or in the air.

UNJAMMING THE TRAFFIC
The reasons for traffic jams are complex. There are too many cars on the roads, but simply building more roads is not the answer. Instead, planners are using the latest computer technology to determine with greater accuracy the reasons for traffic jams. The simulation of traffic patterns (left) takes into account a variety of factors affecting the actual traffic (right). These include changing weather conditions, different types of vehicles and driving styles, breakdowns, and accidents. This information is studied in order to better plan additional roads, control traffic speeds, and provide alternative routes.

This analysis shows the flow of traffic on a busy highway intersection

Getting around

OUR DESIRE TO TRAVEL will not diminish in the 21st century – indeed, it is likely to increase. More people will own cars, so roads will become more congested. We will want to move around the world more quickly, but the skies will be in danger of becoming crowded with aircraft. Attention is now focusing on how to ease these potential problems (pp. 24-25). Train travel will be faster and much more economical, providing passengers and freight with an alternative to jammed highways. And giant airplanes that travel at hypersonic speeds – five times faster than the Concorde – may one day take passengers around the world in a fraction of the time it takes today.

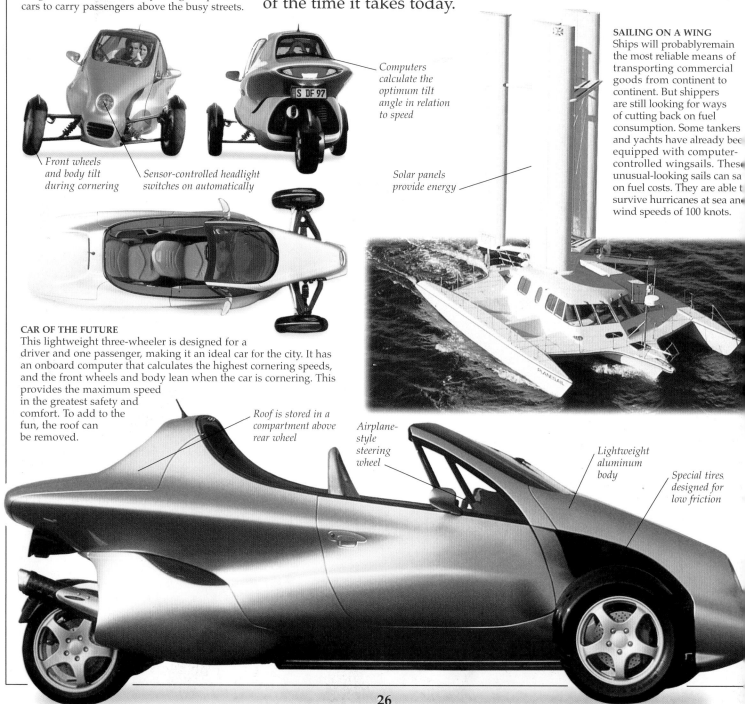

BEAT THE TRAFFIC
This 1923 illustration shows how future urban congestion will be solved by using "torpedo" cars to carry passengers above the busy streets.

Computers calculate the optimum tilt angle in relation to speed

Front wheels and body tilt during cornering

Sensor-controlled headlight switches on automatically

Solar panels provide energy

SAILING ON A WING
Ships will probably remain the most reliable means of transporting commercial goods from continent to continent. But shippers are still looking for ways of cutting back on fuel consumption. Some tankers and yachts have already been equipped with computer-controlled wingsails. These unusual-looking sails can save on fuel costs. They are able to survive hurricanes at sea and wind speeds of 100 knots.

CAR OF THE FUTURE
This lightweight three-wheeler is designed for a driver and one passenger, making it an ideal car for the city. It has an onboard computer that calculates the highest cornering speeds, and the front wheels and body lean when the car is cornering. This provides the maximum speed in the greatest safety and comfort. To add to the fun, the roof can be removed.

Roof is stored in a compartment above rear wheel

Airplane-style steering wheel

Lightweight aluminum body

Special tires designed for low friction

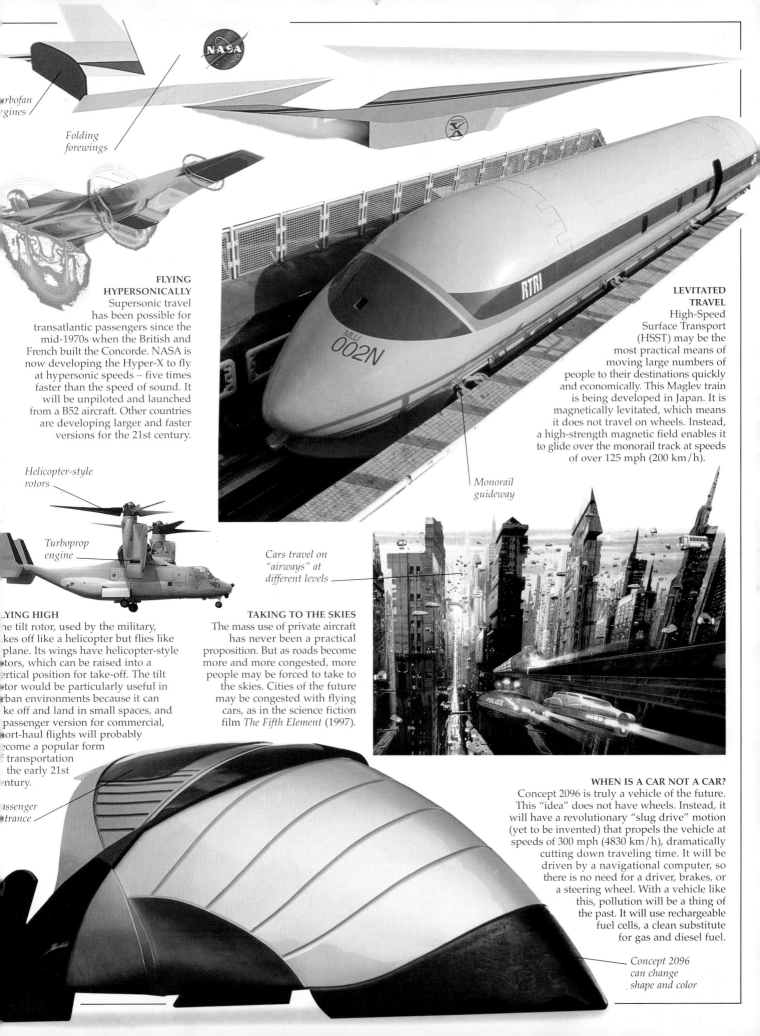

Turbofan engines

Folding forewings

FLYING HYPERSONICALLY

Supersonic travel has been possible for transatlantic passengers since the mid-1970s when the British and French built the Concorde. NASA is now developing the Hyper-X to fly at hypersonic speeds – five times faster than the speed of sound. It will be unpiloted and launched from a B52 aircraft. Other countries are developing larger and faster versions for the 21st century.

Helicopter-style rotors

Turboprop engine

FLYING HIGH

The tilt rotor, used by the military, takes off like a helicopter but flies like a plane. Its wings have helicopter-style rotors, which can be raised into a vertical position for take-off. The tilt rotor would be particularly useful in urban environments because it can take off and land in small spaces, and a passenger version for commercial, short-haul flights will probably become a popular form of transportation in the early 21st century.

Passenger entrance

LEVITATED TRAVEL

High-Speed Surface Transport (HSST) may be the most practical means of moving large numbers of people to their destinations quickly and economically. This Maglev train is being developed in Japan. It is magnetically levitated, which means it does not travel on wheels. Instead, a high-strength magnetic field enables it to glide over the monorail track at speeds of over 125 mph (200 km/h).

Monorail guideway

Cars travel on "airways" at different levels

TAKING TO THE SKIES

The mass use of private aircraft has never been a practical proposition. But as roads become more and more congested, more people may be forced to take to the skies. Cities of the future may be congested with flying cars, as in the science fiction film *The Fifth Element* (1997).

WHEN IS A CAR NOT A CAR?

Concept 2096 is truly a vehicle of the future. This "idea" does not have wheels. Instead, it will have a revolutionary "slug drive" motion (yet to be invented) that propels the vehicle at speeds of 300 mph (4830 km/h), dramatically cutting down traveling time. It will be driven by a navigational computer, so there is no need for a driver, brakes, or a steering wheel. With a vehicle like this, pollution will be a thing of the past. It will use rechargeable fuel cells, a clean substitute for gas and diesel fuel.

Concept 2096 can change shape and color

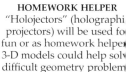

Virtual home in 2020

HOMES OF THE FUTURE will be considerably different from those of the 20th century. They will be energy-efficient and simple to clean and maintain. They will have access to the outside world via a global communications network, making it easy to run a business, do the shopping, and plan a winter vacation, all from the comfort of a living room. There will be an integrated management system, with heating, lighting, and security controls that react to the needs of the occupants. The walls will be constructed from new interactive materials that are able to change appearance at the touch of a button to suit a particular mood, while high-resolution wraparound video screens and holographic projectors will provide fun and entertainment for the whole family.

IDEAL HOME
By the year 2020, some of us might be lucky enough to live in homes with all the latest technology. They will be built from durable materials that require little maintenance. Fully automated, they will react changes in the weather and adjust heating and cooling controls to maintain a pleasant environment.

Scanner in walls of shower connects to health center

POWER SHOWER
A health-and-hygiene station will scan and monitor your well-being while you shower. It will be linked directly to a health center that has a complete record of your family's medical history.

SOMETHING FOR EVERYONE
The dining table will have a multitude of uses. Linked to a communications system, its screens will display newspapers and the latest world news, and allow you to make contact with distant friends and family while you eat.

Interactive screen

Interactive on-line book with flexible screen

"IT'S GOOD TO TALK"
Portable telephones will still be used for business and pleasure, but by the year 2020, they will all be videophones. Increased bandwidth will allow more and more digital information to be sent over the airwaves.

High-resolution video image

HOMEWORK HELPER
"Holojectors" (holographic projectors) will be used for fun or as homework helper 3-D models could help solve difficult geometry problems

It will be possible to take classes via hologram

Nanorobots the size of spiders will roam the carpets, keeping them clean and free of dust

Furniture will be made of special self-cleaning materials

RELAXATION SERVICE
The future family will be able to relax using a therapy couch. Sensitive arms and rollers will gently massage tired body parts, easing away aches and pains. The couch will be linked to a special physiotherapy service, which will give expert advice on health, diet, and exercise.

Screen displays advice

Massage rollers move the length of the couch

Virtual station combines thought control technology with artificial sensory feedback

VIRTUAL REALITY TRAINER
The 2020 home will have its own virtual reality machine. With this, the family will be able to practice dangerous sports such as mountain climbing or bungee jumping, or visit exotic locations on a virtual vacation at the touch of a button.

WRIST SET
Unlike conventional watches, which only tell the time and date or do simple computing tasks, this wrist set will provide information the wearer desires, for example, the sports scores or traffic reports. Such functional electronic gadgets may even replace traditional decorative jewelry.

Clip-on wristband

Walls of house change image to suit mood

VIRTUAL REALITY HEADSETS
In the future, headsets linked to camcorder technology will be able to record your experiences with stereo sound. Using virtual reality headsets, it will be possible to experience 3-D images for pleasure, learning, or business.

Thought recognition sensors

WORK STATION
Working from home is already a popular alternative for many people. In the future, small work stations will provide full access to everything needed to conduct daily business affairs, from e-mail to video conferencing.

Single-function robots have already been designed

ROBOT SERVANTS
Imagine having an addition to the household that always does what it is told. Single-function robots such as vacuum cleaners or lawn trimmers will perform simple tasks around the home. A table that comes to you when it is called will certainly be useful, but it will be better still if it takes away dirty glasses and loads them in the dishwasher.

Chair-based work stations will replace the traditional office

Easy living

IMAGINE STANDING AT a bus stop when, suddenly, your "hot badge" signals that the person behind you likes the same music you do. It might be all you need to know to start a conversation and become friends. Our everyday lives may soon be changed forever because of clever inventions like this one. On these two pages are some ideas of what technology may offer us in the next century. Friendly robots will learn how to perform simple tasks and develop unique personalities. Some jobs, such as shopping or going to the bank, can already be done from home on the Internet, and soon we will be able to consult a doctor in the same way. Travel will be more fun with electronic travel guides and "ear-ins" that translate foreign languages.

SHOP FROM HOME
Shopping from home has been possible for some time, first through mail-order catalogs and then through television. It is only recently that Internet shopping has become popular, although it is not quite like the 1950s image of the future pictured here.

PULL-OUT TRAVEL GUIDE
In the future, finding your way around will be easier with this travel guide. It has a built-in destination planner and provides information about the country you are visiting. The information will be shown on a flexible pull-out screen.

Emotion containers can be any shape or size

Containers are decorative objects

EMOTION CONTAINERS
Emotion containers will be precious gifts. They will be pleasing to look at and made from valuable materials. But they will be much more than that. Each will have a small screen, a loudspeaker, and a scent compartment. The giver of the gift will be able to record a special moment on it, such as a clip from a home video or a baby's first words, for instance. The giver can even include a favorite scent. The moment is captured for the recipient to enjoy.

All you have to do is drop the trash in here

INTELLIGENT GARBAGE CAN
Recycling can be a problem, but in the future dealing with trash will be less messy. The intelligent garbage can is designed to sort trash, keep it from smelling, and make it into compact parcels ready for collection and recycling.

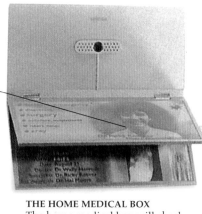

Videophone link with local doctor or hospital

THE HOME MEDICAL BOX
The home medical box will check any symptoms of illness at home, while a handheld computer helps to make a full medical diagnosis. The box has an electronic encyclopedia as well as instruments for measuring temperature, blood pressure, and heart rate. Information can be sent via video link to a local doctor or hospital so that expert medical advice can be given. The box also allows doctors to remotely monitor patients.

Hot badges glow when they "see" a friend

SMART CARDS
Cash will become a thing of the past; carrying smart cards in a wallet will be safer. Fingerprint or voice recognition technology will ensure the card can only be used by its owner. Small credit-card-sized screens will display personal photographs.

Video screen for photographs

MAKING FRIENDS
Hot badges will brighten up your social life. These short-range communication devices are loaded with personal information. They broadcast your personal profile and receive other badges' broadcasts. If two profiles match, the badges will signal their wearers.

EAR-INS
What if hot badges signal that you like the same music, but it turns out that we speak different languages? This will not matter with "ear-ins." These small devices fit snugly into the human ear and can translate simultaneously from one language to another.

Card carries all personal details

Flippin da traxx –
<<turn it up or turn it
off>>

...uchpad

...OUR PERSONAL INTERNET
...his gadget is designed for teenagers. It is a communications ...evice that also gives access to entertainment, like music ...d videos, and information services, such as libraries. It ...ill help with homework projects, but can also be used ...communicate with friends.

This electronic pet will be able to respond to its owner with sound

Electronic pets can be any shape

ELECTRONIC PETS
When we think of robots, we tend to think of the functions they can perform. Robots that can do the washing and ironing or teach you how to play tennis have obvious advantages. But we rarely think of robots as cuddly friends. This is where these robots are different. They are designed to be companions rather than servants. They are capable of responding to emotional needs, and react to voice commands as well as touches or gestures. They have sensors, so they can become familiar with their homes. Like animal pets, they like to be loved.

All in the mind

Sigmund Freud, age 65

BRAIN POWER
For centuries, scientists and philosophers believed that different mental activities could be attributed to specific regions of the brain, as in this 17th-century illustration. However, it is now clear that the regions often depend on each other. While one area of the brain may be crucial for vision, another may be needed to interpret visual information.

THE BRAIN IS THE MOST COMPLEX organ in the human body – and the least understood. Even with today's sophisticated medical technology, our knowledge of how it works remains limited. Brain waves can be measured using an electroencephalograph (EEG). Through a technique known as biofeedback, it is even possible to control and alter brain wave patterns. These changes in signal can then be monitored by a computer and used to operate electronic devices, such as a television screen. The brain also stores our memories and governs our emotions. Understanding people's thoughts and feelings is still the subject of psychological theories, such as psychoanalysis.

However, scientists are also exploring methods for recording life as we experience it by connecting computer chips directly to the brain. Thus, there is the possibility that one day we will record all our thoughts and emotions on a computer chip. A person's experiences will be stored as electronic data for anybody to watch.

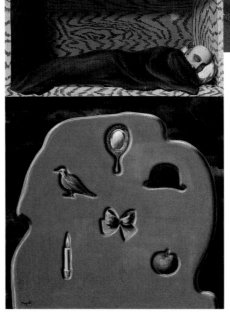

The Reckless Sleeper (1927)

INTERPRETING DREAMS
Sigmund Freud (1856-1939) founded the science of psychoanalysis, a method of analyzing and treating mental illness. He stated that our lives are influenced by both conscious and unconscious thoughts. He believed that through the interpretation of dreams we can gain insight into the unconscious mind.

DREAMS IN ART
Artists have often tried to express the mysteries of the mind through art. Surrealist artist René Magritte (1898-1967) used Freud's theories to explore the unconscious mind through painting.

SLEEP PATTERNS
There are two distinct types of sleep: rapid eye movement (REM) sleep and non-rapid eye movement (NREM) sleep. During REM sleep, there is a great deal of eye, body, and brain activity associated with dreaming. During NREM sleep, eye, body, and brain activity varies. In deep sleep, breathing and heart rate slow down and blood pressure drops. Sleep patterns alternate between periods of REM and NREM.

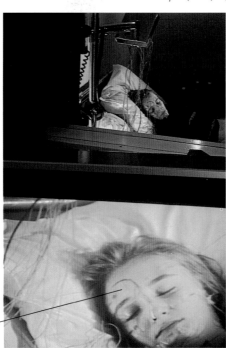

Electrodes connected to monitoring machines measure brain activity

Brain activity of left hemisphere

Brain activity of right hemisphere

REM of left eye

REM of right eye

Heart activity

...EERING POWER

...is woman is steering a flight
...mulator by the power of thought
...ne. Researchers have discovered
...at patterns of brain activity can
... activated by pulsating lights.
... using skilled biofeedback
...hniques, this particular scientist
...n control her brain's response to
... lights. Increased brain activity
...ns the simulator plane right;
...duced brain activity turns it left.

...een line indicates
...vement of plane
...ainst horizon

...ientist
...ntrols
...l in
...mulator

...ND OVER MATTER

...panese scientists have
...oduced a device that
...n detect changes in the
...ta waves produced by
...e mind when it is alert.
...ese changes are picked
..., amplified, and sent
... a computer, which is
...ked to a control panel.
... learning to control the
...ain waves, it is possible
... operate switches
... anything from a
...evision to a central
...ating system.

*Brain activity
of scientist
tunes into
the rhythm
of pulsating
lights*

*Wearer lights up
icon through
concentration*

*Electrode in goggles
picks up changes in
the beta waves*

PERSONALITY TRANSPLANT

This scene from the film *Batman Forever*, in which Jim Carrey receives a thought-wave transplant, may not be entirely imaginary. Scientists are developing a means of connecting nerve endings to microchips. One day, it may be possible to implant memory probes to record and store experiences.

*Different parts of the
brain control different
functions*

INSIDE THE BRAIN

Today's advanced technology allows us to see right inside our own heads and understand more about what is going on there. This computer-generated view of a head with the "lid" taken off shows the parts of the brain that control most complex functions.

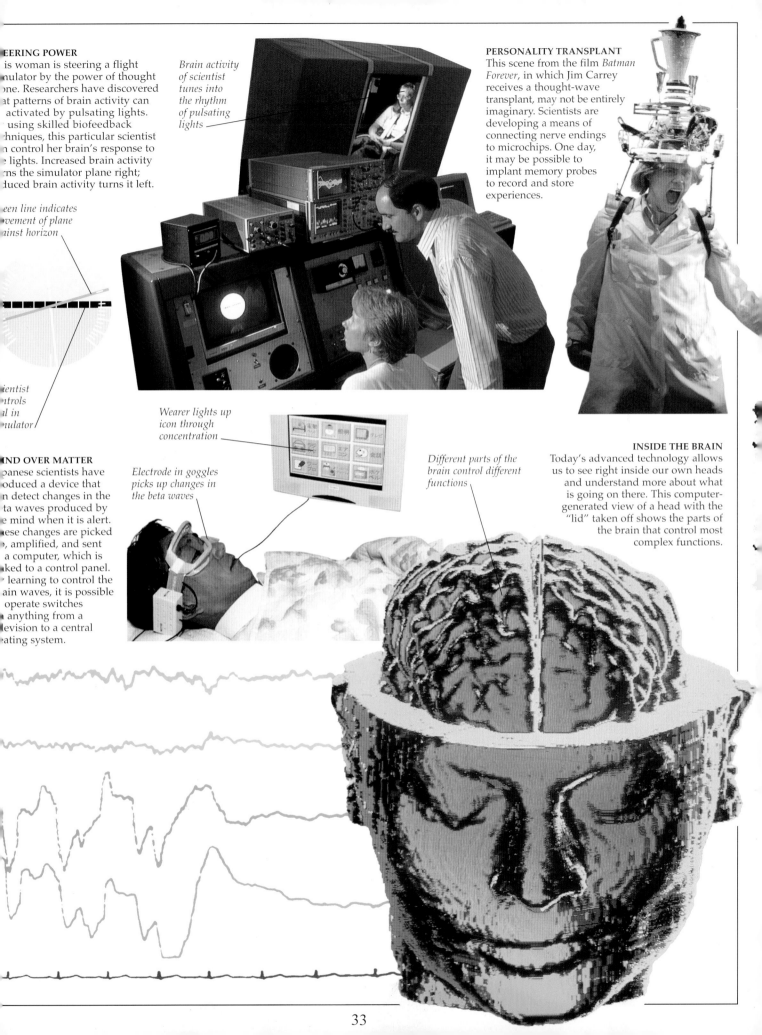

Understanding our bodies

THE HUMAN BODY HAS ALWAYS been mysterious because for so long it was impossible to see exactly how it worked. Anatomists drew the first accurate diagrams from dissected corpses. Then, with the invention of X-rays, it became possible to see through living skin and muscle to the skeleton. Today, doctors use imaging technology to help them monitor patients and diagnose illnesses. Ultrasound is used to observe the progress of a growing fetus inside the womb. Magnetic resonance imaging (MRI) can build three-dimensional images of the interior of the body, allowing doctors to detect diseases. Advances in technology even show us the invisible! Electron microscopes allow us to look into a cell and see the structure of DNA. In the future, we will have a complete record of our genetic makeup.

SUBJECT FOR STUDY
The skeleton is the only part of the human body that does not decay quickly after we die. It defines our shape, allows us to walk upright, and is the frame that supports our body. To understand how it worked, our ancestors had to cut up dead bodies to examine the bones.

THE INNER PERSON
In 1895, German physicist Wilhelm Roentgen took an X-ray of his wife's hand. For the first time, it was possible to look inside the body without cutting the skin. Today, X-rays allow doctors to see the condition of bones and ligaments.

Artwo
of ma
orga
and t
muscu
syste

A computer version of the traditional view of the venous system – the veins of the body – as one continuous vessel

Computer-enhance
view of th
musculoskelet
syster

Computer-generated image of the central nervous system

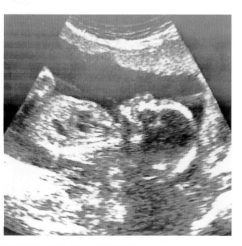

TAKING A LOOK WITH SOUND
The previously hidden world of the womb is made visible through ultrasound. By using ultrasonic waves, it is possible to form images of a fetus growing inside its mother's womb. Ultrasound is also used to examine internal organs.

MAPPING THE BODY
New scanning techniques, such as magnetic resonance imaging (MRI), have made it possible to map the human body very accurately, unlike many of these representations. MRI allows doctors and surgeons to see soft tissue inside the body, such as the brain and spinal cord. By using a powerful magnetic force and radio waves, it is possible to produce a detailed three-dimensional image of the body to aid diagnosis.

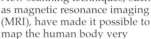

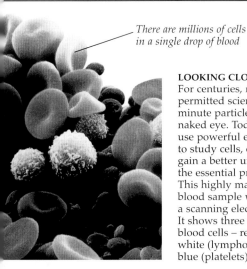

There are millions of cells in a single drop of blood

LOOKING CLOSER
For centuries, microscopes have permitted scientists to look at minute particles invisible to the naked eye. Today, microbiologists use powerful electron microscopes to study cells, enabling them to gain a better understanding of the essential processes of life. This highly magnified image of a blood sample was created using a scanning electron microscope. It shows three common types of blood cells – red (erythrocytes), white (lymphocytes), and blue (platelets).

THE CODE OF LIFE
Deoxyribonucleic acid (DNA) holds the very code of life itself. It is found in the nucleus of every cell and carries genetic information about an individual. The structure of DNA consists of two slender spiral strands that twist around each other to form a shape called a double helix. The strands are held together by compounds known as bases. Scientists around the world are now working together to map the entire sequence of human DNA.

White blood cells do not attack nanorobots, as they are made from a neutral material

NANOROBOTS
The notion of engineering on a minuscule scale was first discussed in the late 1950s. Today, it is becoming a reality. Using high-powered electron microscopes, scientists can examine and manipulate things at the atomic level. They are developing nanorobots – micro-machines that will be small enough to travel through the bloodstream. They will repair or remove diseased tissue at the molecular level. The nanorobots shown in this illustration are destroying diseased tissue inside a human blood vessel.

UNIQUE FINGERPRINTS
In 1984, DNA was internationally recognized as a legal means of identification. Within each person's DNA molecules is a sequence of information unique to that individual (except for identical twins). Forensic scientists are able to identify a chemical sequence (above) to determine whether DNA samples are from the same person. The sequence can be taken from a tiny amount of evidence, such as a single strand of hair or a drop of blood discovered at the scene of a crime.

...norobot's ...nning blades ...troy a tumor

Nanorobot attacks a blood clot

Image is stored in computer

...STANT INFORMATION
...ing a digital camera, a doctor ...kes a photograph of a patient's ...e for his medical records. The ...age can then be displayed on ...omputer screen – and also ...red for future reference. Soon, ...mputerized medical records will ...drawn up for every individual. ...tients visiting the doctor's office ...the hospital will have their ...edical records immediately ...ailable. Eventually, a patient's ...tire medical history, along with ...or her genetic code, will be ...ried everywhere by the patient, ...red on a smart card (pp. 58-59).

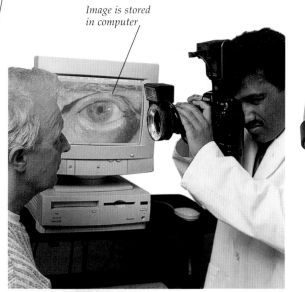

Bases are joined together in complementary pairs

Sequence of bases makes up the cell's genetic code

Several thousand base pairs make up a gene

Model of a DNA double helix

Genetic engineering

ONE OF THE MOST SIGNIFICANT legacies of the 20th century will be the development of our ability to manipulate life through genetic engineering. The human race is poised on the edge of being able to make fundamental changes to the living organisms that share our planet. What would normally take millions of years to develop through the process of natural selection may soon be achieved in a laboratory overnight. One day, geneticists may be able to remove traits from human beings that are considered undesirable for social or medical reasons. They could then replace them with more acceptable characteristics. But this kind of genetic engineering will not only change human biology – it will alter society itself.

MONSTER MYT
Some people fear th
genetic engineering w
produce new monste
like the Chimera
ancient mytholog
which was part lic
part goat, and part snal

PEST CONTROL
By genetically modifying a
virus with a toxin taken fro
a North African scorpion, it
possible to produce a muc|
more effective pesticide
for a worm called the
cabbage looper.
The modified viru
destroys loopers
25 percent faster.

CHEMICAL CODES
The DNA molecule
is composed of units
called nucleotides
that form complicated
sequences. Enzymes are
used to cut sequences to
change something genetically.
Understanding how an enzyme
works allows us to manipulate
the genes.

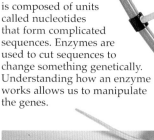

*Patient with cystic
fibrosis must rely
on medical
treatment to
survive*

*Harvard
mouse
specially
engineered
for cancer
research*

GENETIC THERAPY
Congenital disorders,
such as cystic fibrosis or
muscular dystrophy, occur
when a defective gene is
passed on from parents
to their children. These
disorders can result in
a lifelong dependence
on medical treatment
Genetic engineering
offers some hope for
the future. Geneticists
can now isolate the
genes that carry these
diseases. It is hoped
that it will soon be
possible to replace
the defective genes
with healthy ones.

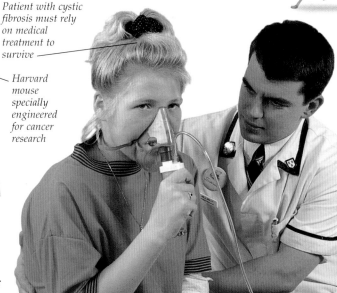

ONE OF A KIND
Genetic engineering may result in research or
business organizations owning life forms. This mouse,
genetically engineered for cancer research at Harvard
University, became the world's first patented mammal
in 1988. Some geneticists argue that if they create a
unique living organism, they should have rights over
its use. However, an international ethical debate has
stalled further patents.

Cloning animals and plants

One of the most incredible, yet troubling, developments of genetic science is the ability to clone animals and plants. A clone is an exact genetic copy of its DNA donor. In 1997, the world was introduced to Dolly the sheep, the first mammal to be cloned from a cell of another adult. Geneticists have already cloned human embryos for medical research. If their techniques are perfected, it may soon be possible to clone human organs and tissue for transplant. However, cloning whole human beings is a controversial issue.

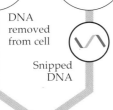
Sheep providing cell

Sheep to be cloned

DNA of sheep to be cloned

DNA removed from cell

Snipped DNA

DNA is fused with cell

New DNA

Cloned embryo is implanted in third sheep

Dolly, the identical copy of DNA donor

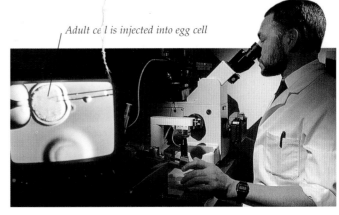
Adult cell is injected into egg cell

SPARK OF LIFE
There are a number of ways of transferring DNA from one cell to another. In Dolly's case, a cell was injected into an egg that had its nucleus removed (above). A spark of electricity fused the cells and promoted growth. Other methods include using bacteria to carry DNA or firing tiny gene-carrying particles into the egg.

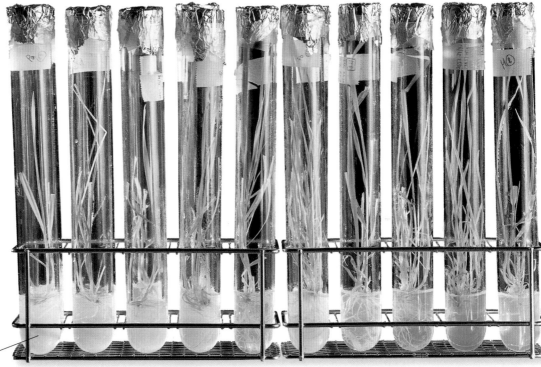
Sterile soil substitute is full of nutrients

THE BIRTH OF DOLLY
The process of creating Dolly involved three sheep. A cell was taken from the first ewe, and its genes were removed. DNA was then taken from a cell of a second ewe and fused with the first cell. Once the embryo was developed, it was implanted into a third sheep, to carry and give birth to Dolly.

Dolly the sheep

PLANT REVOLUTION
Genetic modification has been employed in the farming industry to increase crop yields, improve pest resistance, or boost a crop's ability to thrive in a hostile environment. These cereal plants (above) are clones grown from the single cell of a plant that was genetically modified to produce the desired characteristics.

COUNTLESS CLONES
Cattle have been successfully cloned in the United States, which would permit the mass reproduction of unlimited numbers of identical cows. Cloning cattle would enable farmers to maximize the benefits of desirable traits, such as high milk yields and tender meat. Cows could also be genetically engineered to produce special proteins in their milk for people with specific dietary needs.

Foods of the future?

THE DEMAND FOR FOOD increases daily as the world's population grows. But drought and crop failures have not been eliminated, and pests have become increasingly resistant to insecticides. Meanwhile, sophisticated consumers are demanding fresh food year-round, but they are also concerned about the possible side effects of the chemicals used to increase crop yields. By studying the DNA of plants and animals, scientists hope to revolutionize agriculture. Although there are substantial benefits, the genetic engineering of food remains controversial. Some scientists are concerned that, if they manipulate nature, it may be impossible to reverse any mistakes.

FOOD IN SPACE
There is endless fascination with the food that space travelers eat. In the 1960s, astronauts survived on a diet of dehydrated food and tablets that contained nutritional supplements. Although they were convenient to carry into space, they were not pleasant to eat.

FUTURE FOOD IN SPACE
If one day we choose to live in space, it will be essential to grow food there. This artist's conception of a farming spaceship, shaped like a giant wheel, demonstrates how crops could be grown on a space station. Centrifugal force substitutes for gravity, and the growing crops release oxygen, replenishing the ship's supply.

FUTURE PEST CONTROL
In recent years large amounts of chemical fertilizers, herbicides, and pesticides have been used to protect plants and encourage growth. By genetically modifying crops to be pest-resistant and hardy, it may be possible to eliminate the need for crop spraying.

Potato can be damaged by a cold climate

Flounder with genes that can resist the cold

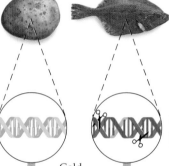

DNA of potato

Cold-resistant gene is cut out of fish DNA

Cold-resistant gene is identified

FISH 'N' CHIPS
A gene from a flounder could be transferred to a potato to make it frost-resistant. The potato could be grown in very cold conditions, benefiting societies living in chilly climates. But people are worried about the long-term effects of exchanging genes between species that could never interbreed naturally.

Gene modification by one of the following methods:
• gene gun
• bacteria
• bursts of electricity or chemicals
• injection

Cold-resistant gene incorporated into potato's DNA

Genetically modified DNA produces a frost-resistant potato

SWEET TOOTH
Those of us who find it hard to resist a slice of chocolate cake may be able to eat as much as we like in the future. Tomorrow's treat will be genetically engineered to be less fattening so we can have our cake without having the fat.

Peanuts can cause a fatal allergic reaction

ALLERGY-FREE NUTS
Most food allergies are slight, and result in no more than a mild rash or stomachache. But some reactions are very severe. The allergic reaction to peanuts, for example, can be particularly serious, causing severe illness or even death. Research is now under way to manipulate the genes of nuts so that all risk of allergic reaction is removed.

ACCELERATED GROWTH
After being genetically modified to produce a growth hormone, this fish is large enough for eating after just 18 months instead of the usual three years. Genetic modification could be the answer to depleting fish stocks. But along with similar experiments on other animals, it raises many serious ethical questions.

BETTER DEAL FOR ALL?

The shelves in supermarkets may soon be filled with genetically modified fruit and vegetables. They will be made to taste better and be more nutritious. They will be longer-lasting, so there will be far less spoilage, which will make them more plentiful and cheaper to buy. Genes that have a negative effect on a certain type of food will be removed and replaced with beneficial ones. And certain fruits and vegetables may also be genetically engineered to defend themselves against harmful viruses, fungi, and insects so they will no longer need to be sprayed with chemical pesticides.

Soft fruits, such as pears and kiwifruit, can be modified to have a longer shelf life in the shops

Bananas can be modified to produce a range of vaccines

Exotic fruits, such as pineapples, can be modified to grow in colder climates

Cauliflowers can be modified to be red or blue to look more appealing

Potatoes can be modified to hold less water so that, when cooked as fries, they will absorb less oil

Strawberries can be modified to be sweeter and juicier

Tomatoes can be modified to withstand common pests, improving their yield 20 to 30 percent

Corn can be modified to resist the corn borer pest, which destroys 20 percent of the corn in Europe

Cabbages and broccoli can be modified to grow well without chemical fertilizers

39

Changing bodies

Oᴜʀ ʙᴏᴅɪᴇꜱ ᴀʀᴇ fragile and complex, vulnerable to disease, and easily damaged. In recent years, medical advances, along with the development of new drugs and materials, have allowed surgeons to replace body parts that are damaged, diseased, or simply worn out. Successful organ transplants mean that people can now survive diseases that twenty years ago would have killed them. Prosthetics (artificial parts) are being developed that give the person wearing them high levels of control, comfort, reliability, and agility. Scientists are also experimenting with implants to combine human cells and microchips, creating physical links between the human body and the latest computer technology. The potential for this work is enormous. One day, implanted machines and computers may mean that the human body will function more efficiently and last longer.

Polyethylene finger joints for arthritis

Titanium and polyethylene elb...

BODY CHIPS
Scientists are developing a method of connecting human nerve cells to a silicon chip. This could counter the effects of brain damage. Already, some forms of blindness have been overcome using semiconductor retinal implants to stimulate the optic nerve.

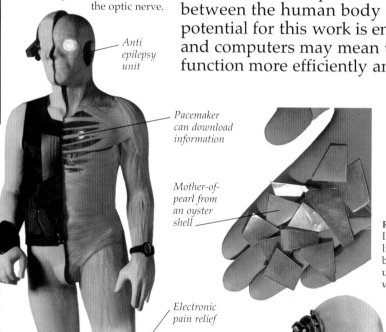

Anti epilepsy unit

Pacemaker can download information

Mother-of-pearl from an oyster shell

Electronic pain relief

Silicon chip controls the mind

Cyborgs are part human, part machine

WIRED MAN
Fictional cyborgs, such as Captain Picard from *Star Trek* (right), with their enhanced strength and superhuman sensory organs, may soon become a reality. In the future, the boundaries between humans and machines will become blurred with the creation of real cyborgs, like the "Wired Man" (above).

FUTURE TRANSPLANTS
Organ transplants are a regular procedure, even among young children. This baby (right) became the youngest person in the world to receive an organ transplant when she was only five days old. Scientists are experimenting with genetically modified animal organs to overcome donor shortages.

REGENERATING BONES
Instead of replacing a damaged limb with a prosthetic, human bone can now be regenerated using mother-of-pearl shell mixed with bone or blood cells (left). When implanted, it stimulates the growth of new bone.

Skin is grown in fibrin gel

NEW SKIN
New skin can be made artificially by placing skin cells in a nutrient-rich gel. The replicating skin cells multiply rapidly – it takes only three weeks to grow into 3.5 sq. ft (1 sq. m.) of new skin. The artificial skin is used on patients who need skin grafts, perhaps after being badly burned.

Titanium and polyethylene implant replaces the toe joint

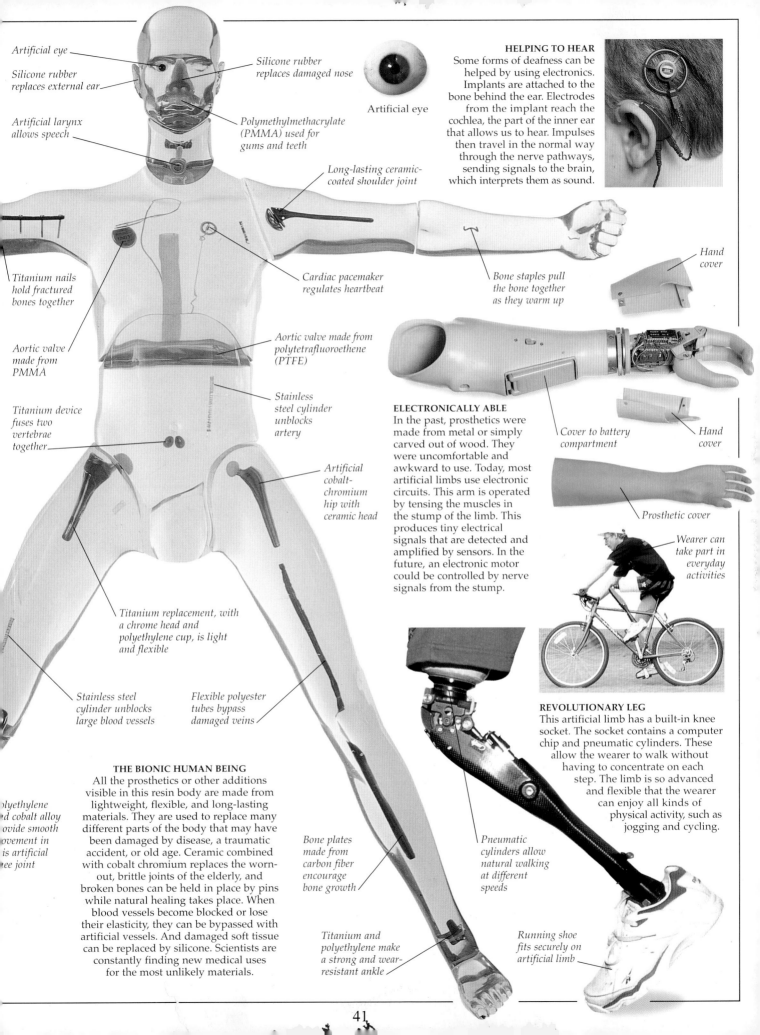

Artificial eye

Silicone rubber replaces external ear

Artificial larynx allows speech

Silicone rubber replaces damaged nose

Polymethylmethacrylate (PMMA) used for gums and teeth

Long-lasting ceramic-coated shoulder joint

Artificial eye

HELPING TO HEAR
Some forms of deafness can be helped by using electronics. Implants are attached to the bone behind the ear. Electrodes from the implant reach the cochlea, the part of the inner ear that allows us to hear. Impulses then travel in the normal way through the nerve pathways, sending signals to the brain, which interprets them as sound.

Titanium nails hold fractured bones together

Cardiac pacemaker regulates heartbeat

Bone staples pull the bone together as they warm up

Hand cover

Aortic valve made from PMMA

Aortic valve made from polytetrafluoroethene (PTFE)

Stainless steel cylinder unblocks artery

Titanium device fuses two vertebrae together

Artificial cobalt-chromium hip with ceramic head

ELECTRONICALLY ABLE
In the past, prosthetics were made from metal or simply carved out of wood. They were uncomfortable and awkward to use. Today, most artificial limbs use electronic circuits. This arm is operated by tensing the muscles in the stump of the limb. This produces tiny electrical signals that are detected and amplified by sensors. In the future, an electronic motor could be controlled by nerve signals from the stump.

Cover to battery compartment

Hand cover

Prosthetic cover

Wearer can take part in everyday activities

Titanium replacement, with a chrome head and polyethylene cup, is light and flexible

Stainless steel cylinder unblocks large blood vessels

Flexible polyester tubes bypass damaged veins

polyethylene d cobalt alloy ovide smooth ovement in is artificial ee joint

THE BIONIC HUMAN BEING
All the prosthetics or other additions visible in this resin body are made from lightweight, flexible, and long-lasting materials. They are used to replace many different parts of the body that may have been damaged by disease, a traumatic accident, or old age. Ceramic combined with cobalt chromium replaces the worn-out, brittle joints of the elderly, and broken bones can be held in place by pins while natural healing takes place. When blood vessels become blocked or lose their elasticity, they can be bypassed with artificial vessels. And damaged soft tissue can be replaced by silicone. Scientists are constantly finding new medical uses for the most unlikely materials.

Bone plates made from carbon fiber encourage bone growth

Pneumatic cylinders allow natural walking at different speeds

REVOLUTIONARY LEG
This artificial limb has a built-in knee socket. The socket contains a computer chip and pneumatic cylinders. These allow the wearer to walk without having to concentrate on each step. The limb is so advanced and flexible that the wearer can enjoy all kinds of physical activity, such as jogging and cycling.

Titanium and polyethylene make a strong and wear-resistant ankle

Running shoe fits securely on artificial limb

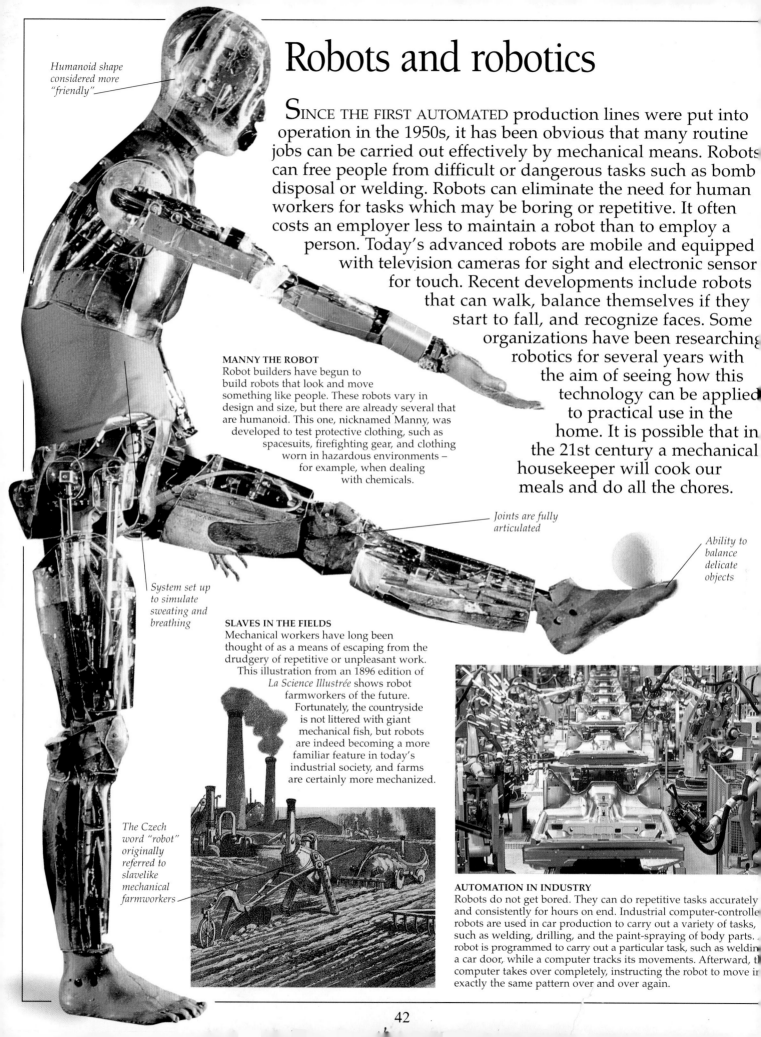

Robots and robotics

SINCE THE FIRST AUTOMATED production lines were put into operation in the 1950s, it has been obvious that many routine jobs can be carried out effectively by mechanical means. Robots can free people from difficult or dangerous tasks such as bomb disposal or welding. Robots can eliminate the need for human workers for tasks which may be boring or repetitive. It often costs an employer less to maintain a robot than to employ a person. Today's advanced robots are mobile and equipped with television cameras for sight and electronic sensors for touch. Recent developments include robots that can walk, balance themselves if they start to fall, and recognize faces. Some organizations have been researching robotics for several years with the aim of seeing how this technology can be applied to practical use in the home. It is possible that in the 21st century a mechanical housekeeper will cook our meals and do all the chores.

Humanoid shape considered more "friendly"

MANNY THE ROBOT
Robot builders have begun to build robots that look and move something like people. These robots vary in design and size, but there are already several that are humanoid. This one, nicknamed Manny, was developed to test protective clothing, such as spacesuits, firefighting gear, and clothing worn in hazardous environments – for example, when dealing with chemicals.

Joints are fully articulated

Ability to balance delicate objects

System set up to simulate sweating and breathing

SLAVES IN THE FIELDS
Mechanical workers have long been thought of as a means of escaping from the drudgery of repetitive or unpleasant work. This illustration from an 1896 edition of *La Science Illustrée* shows robot farmworkers of the future. Fortunately, the countryside is not littered with giant mechanical fish, but robots are indeed becoming a more familiar feature in today's industrial society, and farms are certainly more mechanized.

The Czech word "robot" originally referred to slavelike mechanical farmworkers

AUTOMATION IN INDUSTRY
Robots do not get bored. They can do repetitive tasks accurately and consistently for hours on end. Industrial computer-controlled robots are used in car production to carry out a variety of tasks, such as welding, drilling, and the paint-spraying of body parts. A robot is programmed to carry out a particular task, such as welding a car door, while a computer tracks its movements. Afterward, the computer takes over completely, instructing the robot to move in exactly the same pattern over and over again.

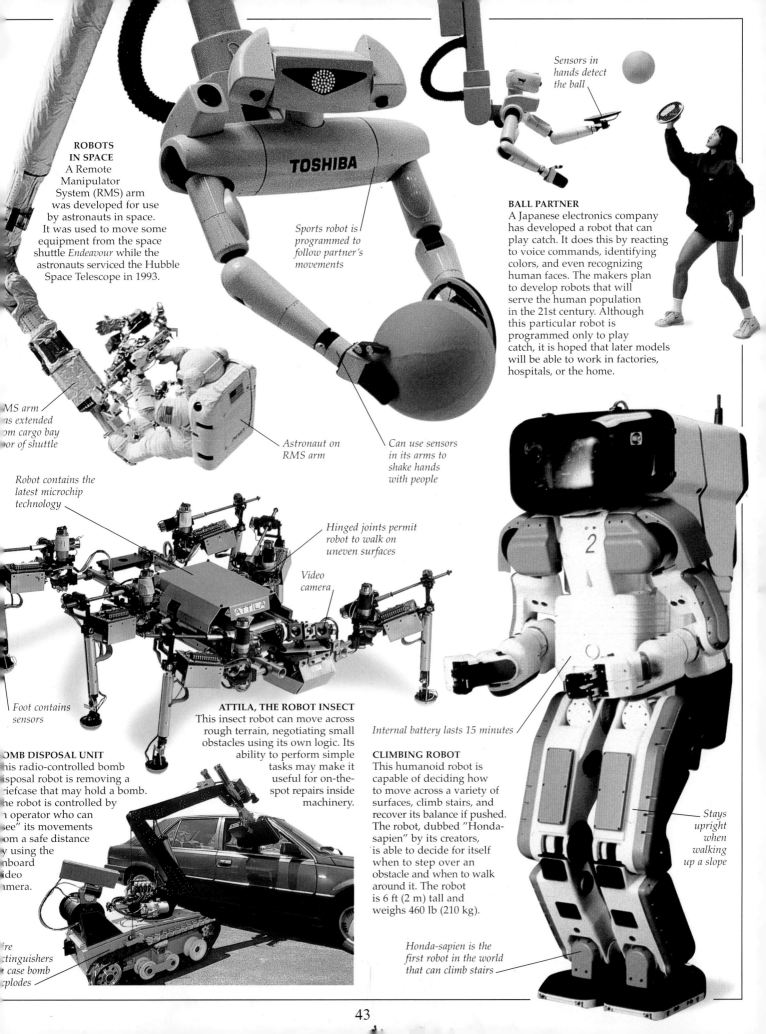

ROBOTS IN SPACE
A Remote Manipulator System (RMS) arm was developed for use by astronauts in space. It was used to move some equipment from the space shuttle *Endeavour* while the astronauts serviced the Hubble Space Telescope in 1993.

Sports robot is programmed to follow partner's movements

Sensors in hands detect the ball

BALL PARTNER
A Japanese electronics company has developed a robot that can play catch. It does this by reacting to voice commands, identifying colors, and even recognizing human faces. The makers plan to develop robots that will serve the human population in the 21st century. Although this particular robot is programmed only to play catch, it is hoped that later models will be able to work in factories, hospitals, or the home.

MS arm as extended om cargo bay or of shuttle

Astronaut on RMS arm

Can use sensors in its arms to shake hands with people

Robot contains the latest microchip technology

Hinged joints permit robot to walk on uneven surfaces

Video camera

Foot contains sensors

ATTILA, THE ROBOT INSECT
This insect robot can move across rough terrain, negotiating small obstacles using its own logic. Its ability to perform simple tasks may make it useful for on-the-spot repairs inside machinery.

Internal battery lasts 15 minutes

OMB DISPOSAL UNIT
his radio-controlled bomb isposal robot is removing a riefcase that may hold a bomb. he robot is controlled by n operator who can ee" its movements om a safe distance y using the nboard ideo amera.

CLIMBING ROBOT
This humanoid robot is capable of deciding how to move across a variety of surfaces, climb stairs, and recover its balance if pushed. The robot, dubbed "Honda-sapien" by its creators, is able to decide for itself when to step over an obstacle and when to walk around it. The robot is 6 ft (2 m) tall and weighs 460 lb (210 kg).

Stays upright when walking up a slope

re tinguishers case bomb plodes

Honda-sapien is the first robot in the world that can climb stairs

Machines that think

MANY PEOPLE BELIEVE that by the middle of the 21st century the world will be populated by "smart" robots, which will be able to make their own judgments and decisions. These robots will be intelligent, independent, and able to communicate with each other. But they will specialize in specific functions, so a robot that can travel at great speeds, for example, will not also be able to play championship chess. However, their skills, overall range of knowledge, and ability to intercommunicate will provide them with great power. Some scientists now predict that robots will become so advanced that they will be able to think for themselves. Robots may one day offer us a life free from drudgery, but such a future is not without risk of creating machines that may take on lives of their own.

ARTIFICIAL INTELLIGENCE TAKES OVER
The science fiction film *2001: A Space Odyssey*, based on the book by Arthur C. Clarke (b.1917), is a story ahead of its time. Today's supercomputers do not yet have the capabilities of the mad computer HAL, which controls the Jupiter-bound spaceship in the film, but it is possible that they will in the future.

Kasparov ponders his next move

The chess computer Deeper Blue

IN DEEP (BLUE) TROUBLE
In 1997, for the first time, IBM chess supercomputer Deeper Blue beat grandmaster Gary Kasparov in a six-game chess match. Kasparov had played a less sophisticated version of the machine before and won, but in Kasparov's own words, this time the computer "suddenly played like a god." Deeper Blue may be capable of analyzing 200 million moves per second and seeing 20 moves ahead, but it cannot run any other software or perform other tasks while playing.

Special sensors check for smoke and humidity

WATCH ROBOT
The Cybermotion SR2 is a security robot used by the Los Angeles County Museum to detect intruders or hazards such as gas, fire, or steam. SR2 navigates the museum without cables or tracks, using a built-in electronic map. It uses sonar to avoid bumping into any of the exhibits, and it communicates with a central computer by radio.

Radio link enables Elma to communicate with computer

ELMA, A ROBOT WITH INSTINCT
Robots ruled by intelligence rather than instructions are being designed by roboticists. Elma, a robot insect built by the Department of Cybernetics at Reading University, England, was constructed solely to learn how to walk. Elma has six independent legs, each of which is operated by its own motor. Elma was preprogrammed by its creators to try out different leg movements. The aim of the experiment was to see if it could move over a surface without falling by coordinating each of its leg movements independently (pp. 46-47).

Central processing brain organizes body-balancing operation

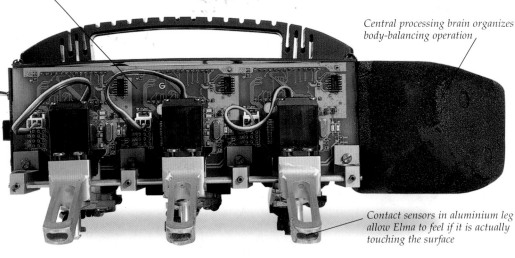

Contact sensors in aluminium leg allow Elma to feel if it is actually touching the surface

Elma at rest

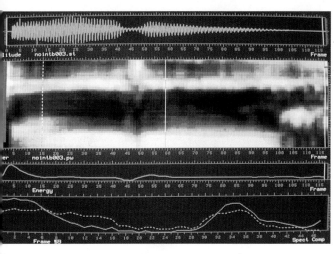

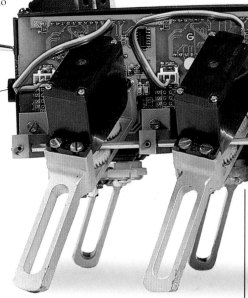

Sensors detect how much force to apply when gripping an object

Artificial tendons generate electrical signals

VOICE RECOGNITION

Computer interfaces still rely heavily on the keyboard and the mouse. This is set to change, as scientists have already begun work on new systems that will allow computers to recognize human voice patterns and understand verbal instructions. The computer graphics seen here represent the speech-synthesized word "baby."

Robot can grip a variety of objects

ROBOT SERVANTS?

A friendly machine doing all the household chores is a popular but unlikely vision of robots in the future. We are a long way from having the technology to create a multi-functional robot with the ability to carry out household duties. Even the simple task of making a cup of tea and delivering it to you in bed is beyond the capabilities of current robots.

APPLYING PRESSURE WITH THE LIGHTEST OF TOUCHES

The human hand is extremely complicated, so it is very difficult to design a machine that can imitate its complex movements. This electrically operated four-fingered robotic hand was designed to investigate force control. The rubber fingertips contain tiny pressure sensors, which can detect how much force is required to grip an object. Information from the sensors is fed to a microprocessor, which is intelligent enough to control the action of all four fingers at once. Instead of muscles and tendons, each finger is operated by wires. Like Elma, the hand can learn from its mistakes, but has no residual memory. Once it is switched off, all that it has learned will be forgotten.

Elma takes a tumble

Elma regains its balance

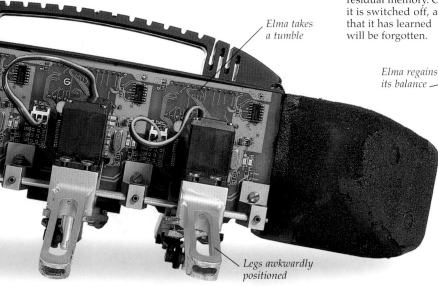

Legs awkwardly positioned

Continued on next page

Artificial intelligence

Scientists and engineers all around the world are trying to build "smart" robots – that is, robots capable of learning. At Reading University, England, robots that can learn how to perform simple functions have been developed. Elma can learn to walk, and wheeled robots known as the Seven Dwarfs are capable of recognizing objects and making decisions about how to move based on this information. The future for robots now lies in their being able to learn from their experiences and pass information on to other robots.

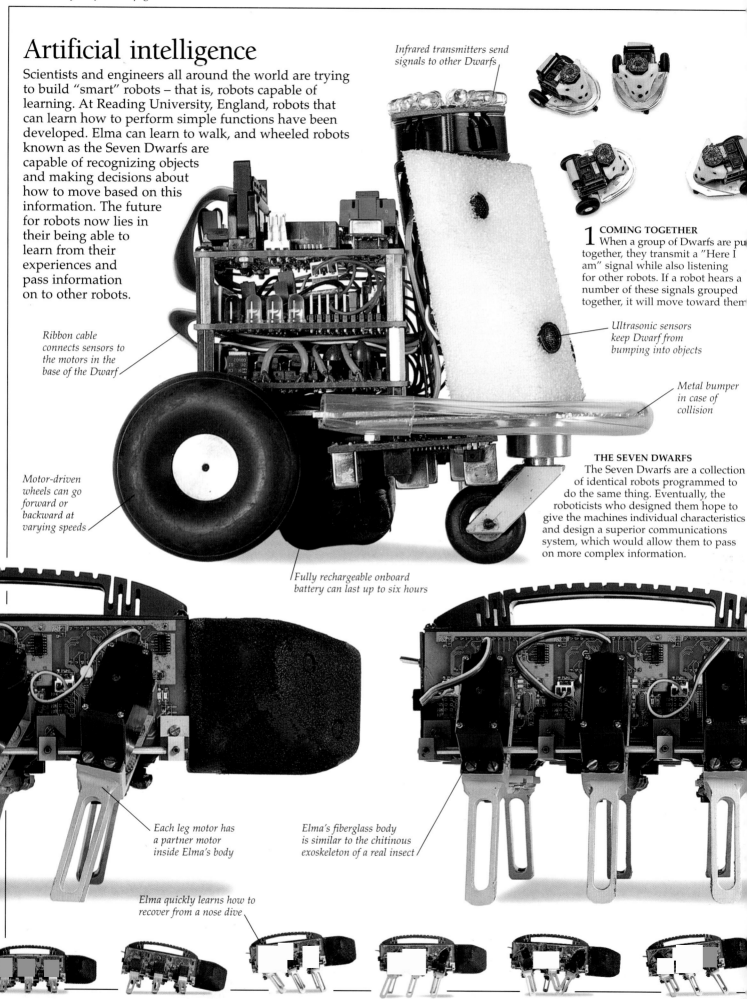

Infrared transmitters send signals to other Dwarfs

1 COMING TOGETHER
When a group of Dwarfs are pu together, they transmit a "Here I am" signal while also listening for other robots. If a robot hears a number of these signals grouped together, it will move toward them

Ultrasonic sensors keep Dwarf from bumping into objects

Ribbon cable connects sensors to the motors in the base of the Dwarf

Metal bumper in case of collision

Motor-driven wheels can go forward or backward at varying speeds

THE SEVEN DWARFS
The Seven Dwarfs are a collection of identical robots programmed to do the same thing. Eventually, the roboticists who designed them hope to give the machines individual characteristics and design a superior communications system, which would allow them to pass on more complex information.

Fully rechargeable onboard battery can last up to six hours

Each leg motor has a partner motor inside Elma's body

Elma's fiberglass body is similar to the chitinous exoskeleton of a real insect

Elma quickly learns how to recover from a nose dive

46

COMMUNICATION
The Dwarfs learn to [av]oid bumping into things, including [ea]ch other. But they are also programmed [to] flock toward each other. They [co]mmunicate efficiently by transmitting [an]d receiving infrared signals.

[Fu]ture operators will be able to [co]ntrol truck from anywhere

NAVLAB II
[T]he Navlab II is a self-driving truck. It is controlled by a [co]mputer called ALVINN (Autonomous Land Vehicle in a [N]eural Network). The computer is "taught" how to drive [b]y a human instructor. Through video cameras and a laser [ra]nge finder, ALVINN can monitor the road and recognize [m]arkings and junctions. Another computer, called EDDIE [(E]fficient Decentralized Database and Interface Experiment), provides additional collision-avoidance software.

[T]HE FUTURE FOR ROBOTS LIKE ELMA
[It] is hoped that, having learned how to walk, Elma [an]d robots like it will be able to navigate a variety of [di]fferent surfaces. Now, Elma is equipped with a radio [li]nk that allows it to communicate directly with a [co]mputer so it can send and receive information about [it]s environment. This information can be used by the [co]mputer to produce a three-dimensional map of the [te]rrain. In the future, robots like Elma will not need [co]mputers, as they will be entirely self-sufficient.

3 GETTING TOGETHER?
The Dwarfs move about, flocking and avoiding each other. When one finds itself with a clear, open space ahead of it, it is programmed to transmit a signal that means "Follow me." The other Dwarfs are programmed to follow and turn to do so.

Computer operator monitors progress of Navlab

Navlab can travel at speeds of up to 37 mph (60 km/h)

Dwarfs learn how to control their wheels to avoid hitting each other and other objects

Each Dwarf transmits its own unique frequency

4 FOLLOW THE LEADER
The latest Dwarfs are programmed to give preference to a leader signal over a group signal. Sometimes more than one leader signal is transmitted at a time, and the group will split, with individual Dwarfs following the nearest signal. When a leader reaches another group, it reverts to using the "Here I am" signal.

Virtual reality

SEEING THE WORLD THROUGH TWO-COLOR GLASSES
Before virtual reality, there was three-dimensional cinema. In the 1950s, members of a 3-D movie audience were each given a pair of cardboard glasses. These were essential – without them the film would look unfocused. Filmmakers designed shots to impress the audience by directing the action toward them. People would duck as objects seemed to fly out from the screen!

Glasses had lenses of different colors

THE EDGES BETWEEN reality and virtual reality are becoming blurred. It is already possible to "experience" an exciting activity such as skiing down a mountain. As computers become more powerful, the virtual experience will become even more real. You will feel the wind in your hair, the frost on your eyebrows, and the gentle heat of the sun on your face, as well as the shudder through your ski boots as you race down the mountain. Virtual reality also has practical uses. It provides us with very beneficial medical applications. Not only can it be used to teach surgical techniques, surgeons are already able to carry out procedures with it, using robotic arms. Imagine the benefits of a surgeon in Australia being able to perform an operation on a patient in Mexico! In the future, virtual reality will be used to train people in many activities, from truck driving and engineering to mountain climbing and atomic physics.

VIRTUAL ENGINEERING
Virtual reality is an effective design tool. It allows manufacturers to model products with a computer instead of having to build expensive prototypes. The people in this picture are viewing a virtual oil rig. A bank of powerful computers, performing a billion operations per second, allows them to be guided through a three-dimensional virtual space to view the oil rig from any angle. The wraparound screen and quadraphonic sound effects complete the spectacle.

"Flychair" has controls that allow the person sitting in it to decide how to "travel" around the oil rig

It is possible to examine complicated machinery in great detail

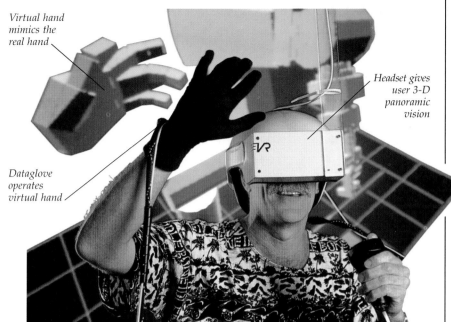

Virtual hand
mimics the
real hand

Headset gives
user 3-D
panoramic
vision

Dataglove
operates
virtual hand

VIRTUAL ENTERTAINMENT
...yet, virtual reality has not been fully developed for
... in the home. Instead, people have "virtual rides" in
...tertainment centers. Here, they watch surfers riding the
...ves in remarkable and nerve-wracking three-dimensional
...lity. In the 21st century, all this will change, with virtual
...lity machines in the home (pp. 28-29) and special virtual
...nsory suits that will allow you to experience the ride itself.

VIRTUAL CONTROL
This visor and glove allow the wearer to interact with a virtual
experience. The glove on his hand provides feedback, allowing him
the sensation of touch. He is programming a virtual reality system
that will be used to control a real robot sent into dangerous situations,
such as the ocean floor or a reactor core in a nuclear power station.

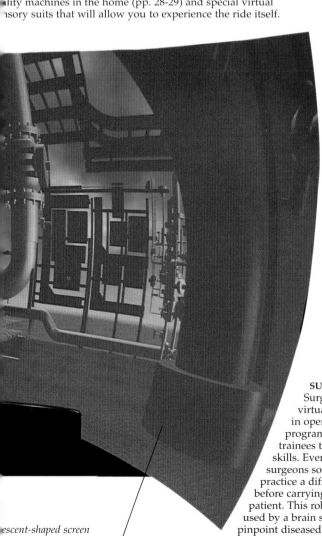

...escent-shaped screen
...s the entire view
...he participants,
...mersing them completely

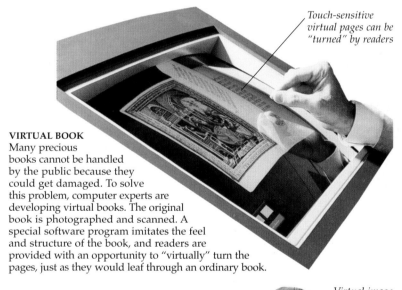

Touch-sensitive
virtual pages can be
"turned" by readers

VIRTUAL BOOK
Many precious
books cannot be handled
by the public because they
could get damaged. To solve
this problem, computer experts are
developing virtual books. The original
book is photographed and scanned. A
special software program imitates the feel
and structure of the book, and readers are
provided with an opportunity to "virtually" turn the
pages, just as they would leaf through an ordinary book.

Virtual image
on screen
shows surgeon
where to
operate

SURGICAL ARM
Surgeons are already using
virtual reality to assist them
in operations. Virtual reality
programs can be used by
trainees to develop their
skills. Even experienced
surgeons sometimes need to
practice a difficult procedure
before carrying it out on the
patient. This robot can be
used by a brain surgeon to
pinpoint diseased areas of
the brain, such as tumors.

Robotic arm
inside a human skull

Seeing the invisible

WITH THE NAKED EYE we can see the world around us, and with a little assistance we can see it more clearly. Eyeglasses help those with poor sight, microscopes allow us to see minute detail, and telescopes permit us to see far into the distance. But there are still many things that remain invisible to us. Visible light is just one small area in a huge electromagnetic spectrum that moves from gamma and cosmic rays through X-rays, ultraviolet radiation, infrared, and microwave, radio waves. Each of these parts of the spectrum allows us to see the world, and the universe, in slightly different ways. Some are familiar but others are just being discovered. X-rays have been used in medicine for more than a century. Radar was first used in World War II to locate enemy aircraft and ships. Today, ultraviolet light can be used to help drivers to see better at night, while space telescopes are sending back spectacular images from deepest space.

X-RAY SPECS
Children had fun with these pretend X-ray specs (or gogs), launched in the 1950s. They could use their imagination to pretend they were spies or secret agents, capable of seeing through the walls of buildings, or even through skin to their own skeleton. If one day in the future X-ray specs do become a reality, they would certainly be used by everyone.

View of road ahead with ordinary headlights

View of road ahead with ultraviolet headligh

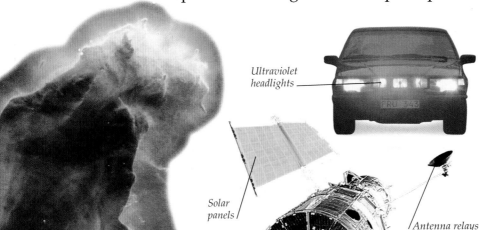

Ultraviolet headlights

Solar panels

Antenna relays data back to Earth via radio

OUT IN SPACE
We can now look out into space and see the birth of stars. The Hubble Space Telescope was launched in 1990 to look at the optical and ultraviolet universe. In 1995, it sent back the first high-quality images of the Eagle Nebula (left), a huge cloud of gas and dust 7,000 light-years from Earth.

Columns of hydrogen gas act as incubators for new stars

VISION
It is hardly surprising that most ro accidents occur at night. In poor visibil a driver has far less warning of a haz ahead, and therefore less time to avoid Brighter headlights are not practical becau they dazzle oncoming traffic. But ultraviol light, invisible to the human eye, can used. It reflects off fluorescent mater warning the driver in time to st

Contents of tr visible on scr

SECURITY CHECK
Customs officials at airports and ports throughout the world use X-ray machines to check the contents of luggage. With new technology, larger and more sophisticated machines have been designed that are capable of checking the entire contents of vehicles, such as this truck (right). Previously it could take anywhere up to 24 hours to carry out a security check – now it can be done in a matter of minutes.

VIEW FROM SPACE
This color-enhanced image of an earthquake was taken by the *ERS-1* satellite. It is the first view of an earthquake from space and shows how the ground was displaced in California in 1992. The closer the color bands are, the greater the ground displacement.

Colored bands show shockwaves of earthquake

...ot's cabin

...EALTH FIGHTER
...is difficult to make ...mething as large as an ...rplane disappear, but that is ...at Lockheed attempted to do ...th their F-117 Stealth Fighter. ... angular shape deflects radar ...ams, making it difficult to spot ...d almost impossible for guided ...ssiles to attack. Although the fighter ...n be cloaked from radar, it is not ...visible to other detection devices, such ... thermal imaging.

Security officials can see through 11 in (28 cm) of steel, revealing any secret cargo

Angular shape deflects radar beams

OCEAN FLOOR
This sonar image taken of the sea bed in the Gulf of Mexico was made by ships recording sound echoes from the ocean floor. The different colors show the various depths. Buried rock sediment, deposited from the Mississippi River, creates a crater landscape that resembles the surface of the moon.

Infrared goggles give soldier ability to see in the dark

TOMORROW'S KILLING MACHINE
Camouflage has been used to help soldiers and their weaponry blend into the background. However, the use of radar, ultra-sensitive listening devices, and thermal imaging makes it increasingly difficult for soldiers to "disappear." Military scientists are developing new cloaking devices so that soldiers and their equipment can hide from enemy targets.

Heads-up display (HUD) projects tactical information into eyepiece

"Smart" weapon includes a laser to pick out target

Getting smaller

THE INVENTION OF THE TRANSISTOR in 1947, and its successor, the integrated circuit, in 1959, has transformed our world. Previously, the cumbersome vacuum tubes used in radios and television sets generated a lot of heat and had to be housed in large containers. Today, thousands of electrical components are etched onto tiny wafers of silicon to make microprocessors. This technology has spawned a computer industry that only a few years ago was unimaginable, with powerful hand-held computers that can be linked to satellites to provide e-mail and Internet access. In the past, a radio smaller than a mouse seemed unimaginable, but now one exists. In the future, components will get even smaller still.

IN MINIATURE
The integrated circuit is an essential feature of modern technology. It replaced the diverse separate components of early electronics. Many thousands of individual transistors can be carried on a tiny chip of silicon, changing the look and the way electronics can be applied.

COMPACT EARPHONES
Compact, portable cassette machines became widely available in the 1980s. Their high-quality sound was played back through small headphones. These have since been replaced by even smaller earpieces that fit right inside the ear.

POWER SUPPLY
These tiny, lightweight batteries can be used to power a whole range of electronic equipment, from watches to cameras.

ENIAC had to be rewired each time it was programmed

MONSTER MACHINE
Before the introduction of transistors and integrated circuits, scientists relied upon valve technology for their electronic computers. This meant that computers were extremely large and not very powerful. One of the first computers, ENIAC, weighed 30 tons and occupied a whole room.

RECORDING IN MINIATURE
The latest compact discs (above) can store sound, graphics, and moving images. Although they are small, they have a large memory capacity. Now you can also record your own music on the tiniest of cassettes (left), with a quality of sound that is ten times better than when cassettes were invented in the 1970s.

PALM-TOP COMPUTER
In less than 50 years, computers have been reduced in size so that now they can fit into the palm of your hand. The Psion may be small, but it is extremely powerful. It contains a personal organizer, a database, and a word processor, and it is programmable. It can also send and receive messages, access the Internet, and exchange e-mail – all in the palm of your hand.

Modem connection

Fully functional keyboard

Back batter for da storag

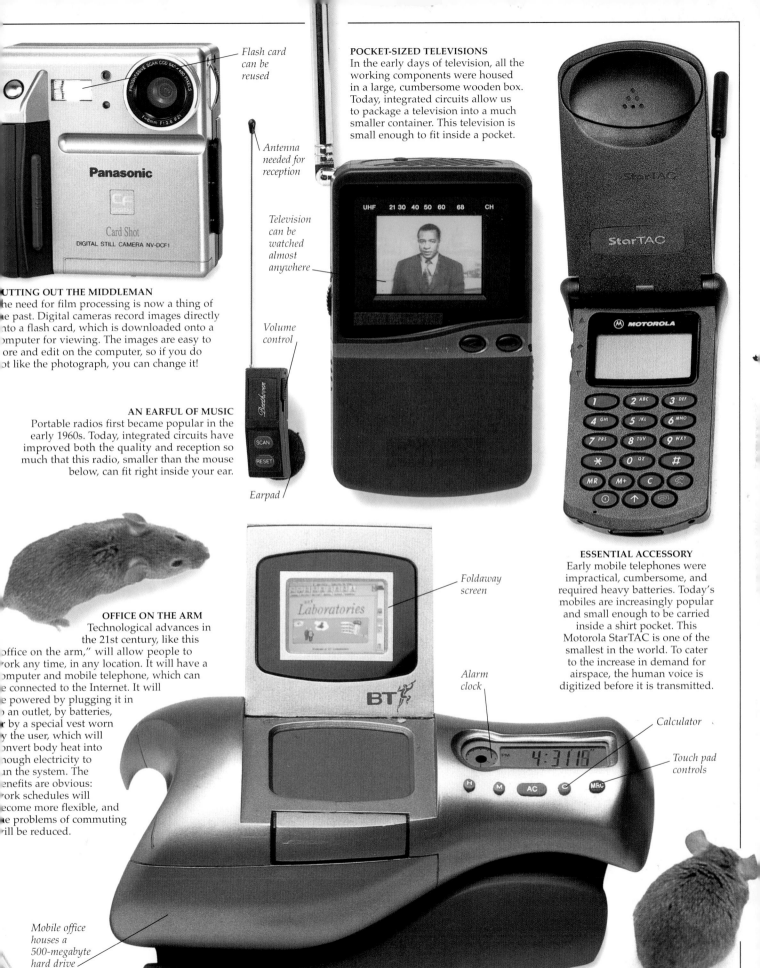

Flash card can be reused

POCKET-SIZED TELEVISIONS
In the early days of television, all the working components were housed in a large, cumbersome wooden box. Today, integrated circuits allow us to package a television into a much smaller container. This television is small enough to fit inside a pocket.

Antenna needed for reception

Television can be watched almost anywhere

UHF 21 30 40 50 60 68 CH

Volume control

UTTING OUT THE MIDDLEMAN
he need for film processing is now a thing of e past. Digital cameras record images directly nto a flash card, which is downloaded onto a omputer for viewing. The images are easy to ore and edit on the computer, so if you do ot like the photograph, you can change it!

AN EARFUL OF MUSIC
Portable radios first became popular in the early 1960s. Today, integrated circuits have improved both the quality and reception so much that this radio, smaller than the mouse below, can fit right inside your ear.

SCAN

RESET

Earpad

MOTOROLA

1 2 ABC 3 DEF
4 GHI 5 JKL 6 MNO
7 PRS 8 TUV 9 WXY
* 0 QZ #
MR M+ C
I ↑

ESSENTIAL ACCESSORY
Early mobile telephones were impractical, cumbersome, and required heavy batteries. Today's mobiles are increasingly popular and small enough to be carried inside a shirt pocket. This Motorola StarTAC is one of the smallest in the world. To cater to the increase in demand for airspace, the human voice is digitized before it is transmitted.

OFFICE ON THE ARM
Technological advances in the 21st century, like this office on the arm," will allow people to ork any time, in any location. It will have a omputer and mobile telephone, which can e connected to the Internet. It will e powered by plugging it in o an outlet, by batteries, r by a special vest worn y the user, which will onvert body heat into nough electricity to un the system. The enefits are obvious: ork schedules will ecome more flexible, and e problems of commuting ill be reduced.

Foldaway screen

Laboratories

BT

Alarm clock

Calculator

Touch pad controls

4:37

H M AC C MRC

Mobile office houses a 500-megabyte hard drive

Lighter than air

NEW MATERIALS ARE being developed all the time. The invention of plastic in the early 20th century revolutionized our world, and plastic became the lightweight alternative to traditional materials such as wood, metal, and glass. There are now hundreds of different types of plastic, and others are being developed. Plastics are very adaptable and can be used to make anything from durable toys to pliable contact lenses. However, most plastics are not biodegradable, so millions of tons of wasted plastic cannot be disposed of safely. New materials and processes may provide solutions, but in the meantime, scientists are developing more environmentally friendly materials for the next millennium. Some lightweight synthetics are stronger than steel, yet they can be woven into clothing. Foamed metals use fewer raw materials, making them lighter but still just as strong.

BUCKYBALLS
Buckyballs are tiny spherical structures made up of 60 carbon atoms. They may become the building blocks of a new kind of engineering at a molecular level – creating nanomachines (pp. 34-35).

HEAT-RESISTANT TILES IN SPACE
Silica tiles line the underside of the space shuttle *Columbia*. The heat-dissipating tiles are made from a high-quality sand, and are used to protect the shuttle from the extreme temperatures as it re-enters the Earth's atmosphere.

Carbon cotton feels rougher than normal cotton

Pull a carbon thread as hard as you like – you can't break it

LIGHTWEIGHT FRAME
Designed by Lotus Cars, this lightweight automobile chassis is a remarkable piece of engineering. It only weighs 149 lbs (68 kg) – half the usual steel equivalent – and can be easily lifted by two men. It is made from an alloy that is sensitive to heat. Instead of welding, the metal joints are held together by a powerful glue.

Rivets keep joints from coming apart

Bonded chassis is both lightweight and strong

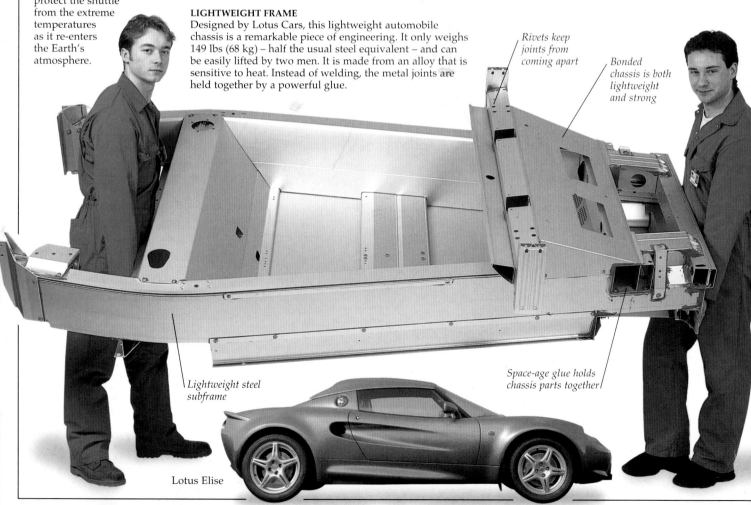

Lightweight steel subframe

Space-age glue holds chassis parts together

Lotus Elise

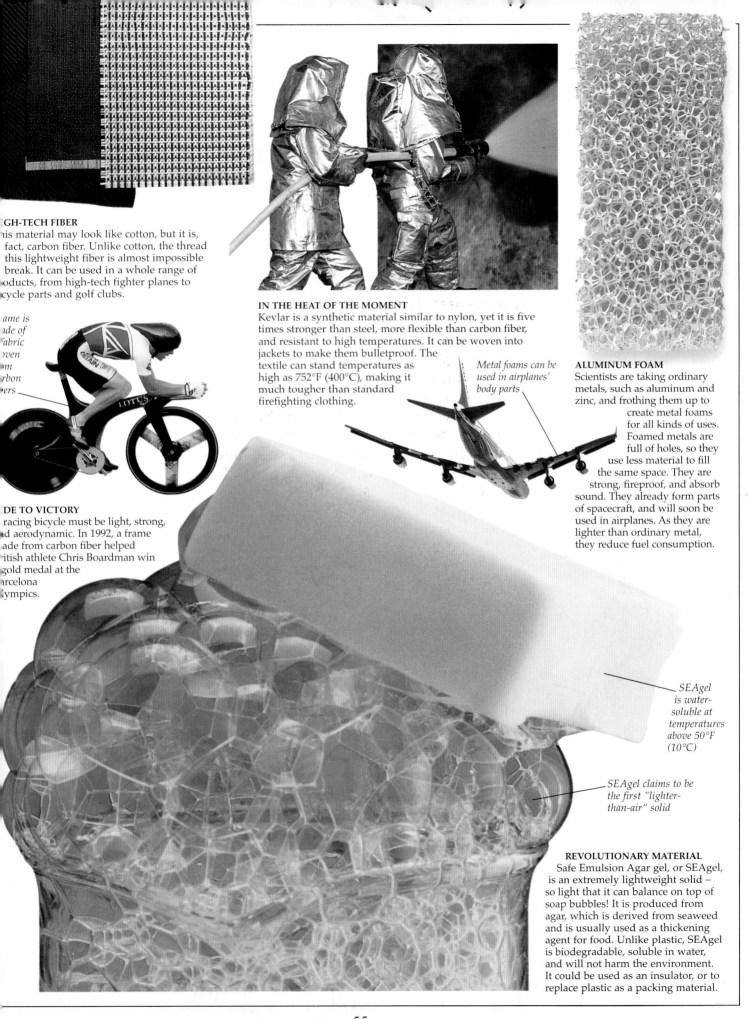

HIGH-TECH FIBER
This material may look like cotton, but it is, in fact, carbon fiber. Unlike cotton, the thread of this lightweight fiber is almost impossible to break. It can be used in a whole range of products, from high-tech fighter planes to bicycle parts and golf clubs.

The frame is made of fabric woven from carbon fibers

RIDE TO VICTORY
A racing bicycle must be light, strong, and aerodynamic. In 1992, a frame made from carbon fiber helped British athlete Chris Boardman win a gold medal at the Barcelona Olympics.

IN THE HEAT OF THE MOMENT
Kevlar is a synthetic material similar to nylon, yet it is five times stronger than steel, more flexible than carbon fiber, and resistant to high temperatures. It can be woven into jackets to make them bulletproof. The textile can stand temperatures as high as 752°F (400°C), making it much tougher than standard firefighting clothing.

Metal foams can be used in airplanes' body parts

ALUMINUM FOAM
Scientists are taking ordinary metals, such as aluminum and zinc, and frothing them up to create metal foams for all kinds of uses. Foamed metals are full of holes, so they use less material to fill the same space. They are strong, fireproof, and absorb sound. They already form parts of spacecraft, and will soon be used in airplanes. As they are lighter than ordinary metal, they reduce fuel consumption.

SEAgel is water-soluble at temperatures above 50°F (10°C)

SEAgel claims to be the first "lighter-than-air" solid

REVOLUTIONARY MATERIAL
Safe Emulsion Agar gel, or SEAgel, is an extremely lightweight solid – so light that it can balance on top of soap bubbles! It is produced from agar, which is derived from seaweed and is usually used as a thickening agent for food. Unlike plastic, SEAgel is biodegradable, soluble in water, and will not harm the environment. It could be used as an insulator, or to replace plastic as a packing material.

New frontiers

THROUGHOUT HISTORY, HUMANS have been driven to explore the far reaches of the globe in search of valuable minerals and new forms of life. Now that there are few areas of the world left unexplored, our sights have risen beyond our own planet and into space itself. Only a few centuries ago wooden ships powered by the wind traveled across the oceans into uncharted territories. In an echo of this recent history, we will in the future send spaceships powered by the solar wind to explore space. We will colonize planets and perhaps discover other forms of life. But we cannot rely on Earth to provide the materials to build and power these missions. Asteroids will be mined for resources, and huge solar power satellites will be built to generate electricity. Only then can colonies be established on the moon and nearby planets.

FLY ME TO THE MOON
Vacations in space first captured people's imagination in the 1950s, when we were on the brink of sending the first human being into orbit. In the 21st century, there will be bases on the moon, probably with busy lunar hotels.

Mining the asteroids

MINING THE UNIVERSE
The moon and asteroids are very rich in natural resources – minerals such as gold, platinum, nickel, and iron have already been identified. Moon dust contains hydrogen, which could be used to power rockets, as well as helium-3, a potential fuel for fusion reactors. One day, the moon and asteroids will be mined for raw materials, which will be used either for deeper space travel or sent back to Earth in huge solar-powered freighters. Asteroids might even be towed closer to the Earth, making it easier to exploit their enormous mineral wealth.

Mining the moon

Structure molded out of Mars rock

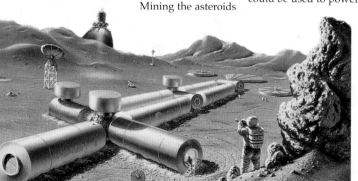

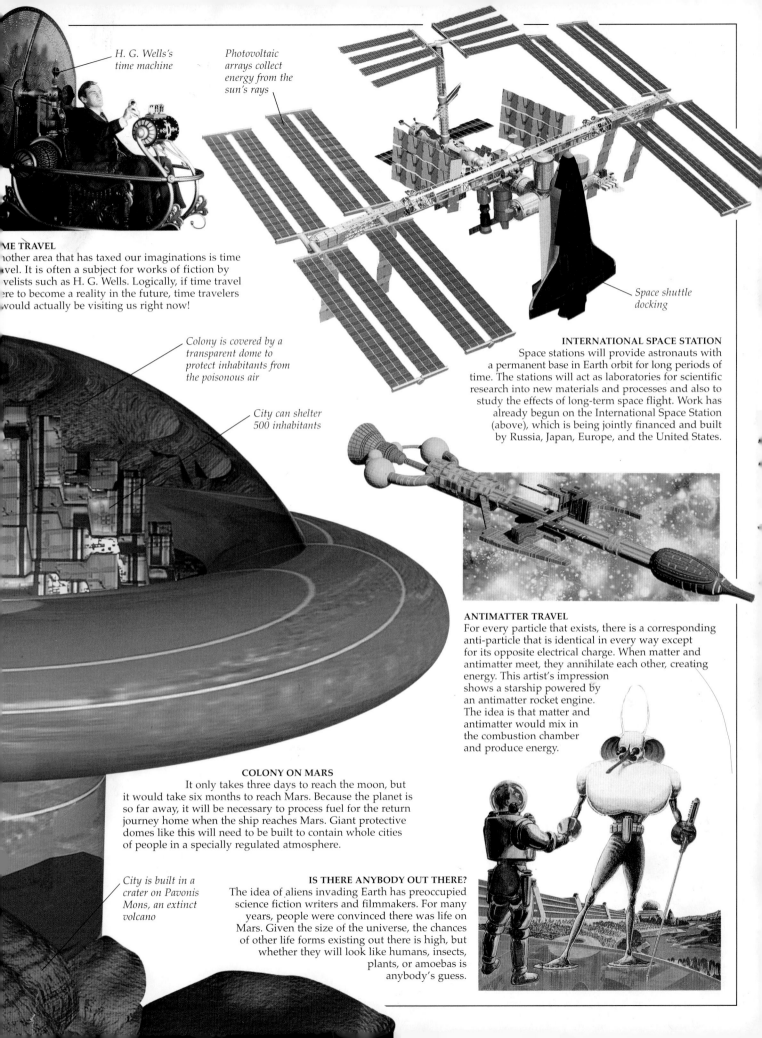

H. G. Wells's
time machine

Photovoltaic
arrays collect
energy from the
sun's rays

[TI]ME TRAVEL

[A]nother area that has taxed our imaginations is time
[tra]vel. It is often a subject for works of fiction by
[no]velists such as H. G. Wells. Logically, if time travel
[we]re to become a reality in the future, time travelers
[would actually be visiting us right now!

Space shuttle
docking

Colony is covered by a
transparent dome to
protect inhabitants from
the poisonous air

City can shelter
500 inhabitants

INTERNATIONAL SPACE STATION

Space stations will provide astronauts with
a permanent base in Earth orbit for long periods of
time. The stations will act as laboratories for scientific
research into new materials and processes and also to
study the effects of long-term space flight. Work has
already begun on the International Space Station
(above), which is being jointly financed and built
by Russia, Japan, Europe, and the United States.

ANTIMATTER TRAVEL

For every particle that exists, there is a corresponding
anti-particle that is identical in every way except
for its opposite electrical charge. When matter and
antimatter meet, they annihilate each other, creating
energy. This artist's impression
shows a starship powered by
an antimatter rocket engine.
The idea is that matter and
antimatter would mix in
the combustion chamber
and produce energy.

COLONY ON MARS

It only takes three days to reach the moon, but
it would take six months to reach Mars. Because the planet is
so far away, it will be necessary to process fuel for the return
journey home when the ship reaches Mars. Giant protective
domes like this will need to be built to contain whole cities
of people in a specially regulated atmosphere.

City is built in a
crater on Pavonis
Mons, an extinct
volcano

IS THERE ANYBODY OUT THERE?

The idea of aliens invading Earth has preoccupied
science fiction writers and filmmakers. For many
years, people were convinced there was life on
Mars. Given the size of the universe, the chances
of other life forms existing out there is high, but
whether they will look like humans, insects,
plants, or amoebas is
anybody's guess.

Living in the future

ALL AROUND US developments are taking place that will dramatically affect our lives. Molecular scientists are uncovering the fundamental processes of life itself. The inherited characteristics of our descendants may one day be in the hands of genetic engineers. If research into robotics is successful, we may share our planet with intelligent machines. New materials are being developed all the time. Our future may not even be on this planet. Wherever it is, and whatever it is like, it is yours to find out about, take part in, and enjoy!

CITIES OF THE FUTURE
The dream of cities in space may soon become a reality. Ice discovered at the moon's polar regions could be used to manufacture fuel and oxygen. This will provide the raw materials to build the first small space colonies.

GROWING POPULATION
Growth in the world's population increases demand on resources. International cooperation will be needed to ensure fair distribution and manage the environment.

Smart card microchip will carry information

UTOPIA National Identification Card
Cedula de Identidad
Name/Nombre
MARIA GONZALEZ
Sex/ Nationality/ Date of Birth/
Sexo Nacionalidad Fecha de Nacimiento
F UTO 12 JUL 57
Doc No/N.º de Doc Expires/Vencimiento
D23145890 12 JUL 97
Maria Gonzalez
...ad West
...N 55440

I<UTOD231458907<<<<<<<<<<<<<<<
3407127M9507122UTO<<<<<<<<<<<<8
MARIA<GONZALEZ<<<<<<<<<<<<<<<<<

"SMART" CARDS
Your full personal history could soon be recorded on a smart card. Combining a driver's license, a passport, medical records, financial status, and employment and criminal records, it will be used for all transactions.

MECHANICAL SERVANTS
Robots will require massive computing power if they are to assist us in all aspects of our everyday lives. We are likely to create machines more intelligent than ourselves, "smart" robots with the ability to make up their own minds.

VIRTUAL REALITY
Virtual reality is destined to make a significant impact on the way we live. We are now able to watch motor racing from the stands. In the future, we will be able to take "virtual" part in the race itself. Doctors will routinely use virtual reality to assist with their operations, while scientists, like this physicist, will use it to design experiments or work out theories.

NEW MATERIALS
New technology will alter our relationship with the physical world. Materials that can change shape could be used to make products less prone to damage. In building, materials could be instructed to change shape if, for example, the area is hit by an earthquake.

Glasses apparently crushed and unusable

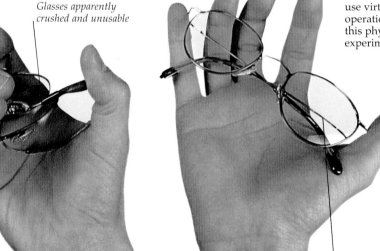

Glasses "remember" their shape

DESIGNING LI...
Molecular biology will pl... a significant role in the ne... century. The discovery... DNA and the developme... of genetic engineeri... mean that we are able... manipulate life at a bas... level. But this raises t... question of how mu... we should interfe...

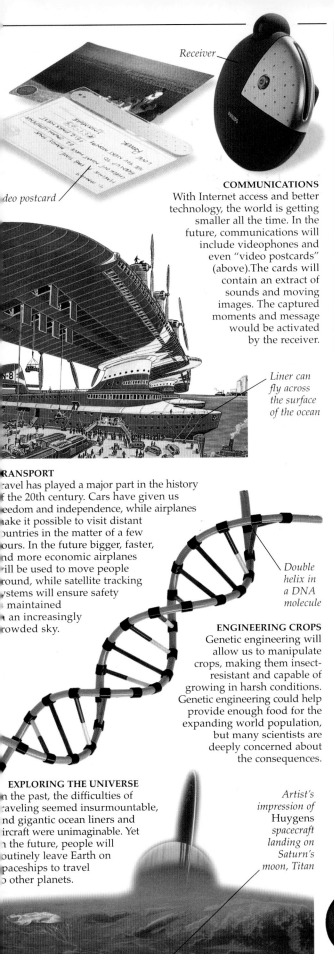

Receiver

Video postcard

COMMUNICATIONS
With Internet access and better technology, the world is getting smaller all the time. In the future, communications will include videophones and even "video postcards" (above). The cards will contain an extract of sounds and moving images. The captured moments and message would be activated by the receiver.

Liner can fly across the surface of the ocean

TRANSPORT
Travel has played a major part in the history of the 20th century. Cars have given us freedom and independence, while airplanes make it possible to visit distant countries in the matter of a few hours. In the future bigger, faster, and more economic airplanes will be used to move people around, while satellite tracking systems will ensure safety is maintained in an increasingly crowded sky.

Double helix in a DNA molecule

ENGINEERING CROPS
Genetic engineering will allow us to manipulate crops, making them insect-resistant and capable of growing in harsh conditions. Genetic engineering could help provide enough food for the expanding world population, but many scientists are deeply concerned about the consequences.

EXPLORING THE UNIVERSE
In the past, the difficulties of traveling seemed insurmountable, and gigantic ocean liners and aircraft were unimaginable. Yet in the future, people will routinely leave Earth on spaceships to travel to other planets.

Artist's impression of Huygens spacecraft landing on Saturn's moon, Titan

Calendar of the future
Imagine traveling in a time machine into the middle of the 21st century. What do you think life will be like then? By examining current developments, it is possible to make predictions about the future. Many of these predictions may happen and some may not, but those marked with asterisks could happen at any time.

2001	Common use of solar cells for residential power supply
2001	Wall-hung high-definition color displays
2001	Electronic newspapers and paintings
2001	Hand videophone
2001	Home shopping via Internet
2001	Artificial blood and ears
2001	Full personal medical records stored on smart card
2004	Electronic notebook as readable as paper
2005	Hydraulic chair for virtual reality games
2005	Various forms of electronic addiction become a problem
2006	Tactile sensors comparable to human sensation
2007	Global electronic currency in use
2007	Determination of whole human DNA base sequence
2007	Robotized space vehicles and facilities
2009	Firefighting robots that can find and rescue people
2010	Smart clothes that can alter their thermal properties
2011	Multilayer solar cells with efficiency greater than 50 percent
2011	Robotic security and fire guards
2011	Housework robots to fetch, carry, clean, tidy, and organize
2014	Nanorobots roaming in blood vessels under own power
2014	Robotic pets
2014	Electronic shopping dominant
2014	First human landing on Mars
2020	3-D videoconferencing
2020	Genetic links of all diseases identified
2020	Artificial lungs, kidneys, and brain cells
2020	Cars that drive themselves on smart highways
2025	Deep underground cities in Japan
2025	New forms of plants and animals from genetic engineering
2025	Artificial liver
2025	Extension of lifespan to over 100
2025	Flying-wing planes carry passengers at 600 mph (960 km/h)
2030	More robots than people in developed countries
2035	Fully functioning artificial eyes and legs
**	Collapse of the world's fisheries
**	Asteroid hits Earth
**	Unknown long-term side effects of medications discovered
**	Viruses become immune to all known treatments
**	International financial collapse
**	Major information disruption
**	Nanotechnology takes off
**	Energy revolution
**	Collapse of the United Nations
**	Terrorism rises beyond the capability of government systems
**	First unambiguous contact with extraterrestrial life
**	Human mutation
**	Worldwide epidemic
**	Time travel invented

Video watch

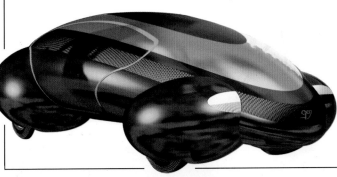

Self-driving car of the future

Index

Acknowledgments

Dorling Kindersley would like to thank:
Professor Kevin Warwick, Michael Hilton, Darren Wenn, and Dr David Keating of the Department of Cybernetics, University of Reading (pp. 44–47); Alistair Florence, Carol Highmoor, Paul Fleming and Darren Cockle of Lotus Cars (pp. 54–55); Gary Dalton, Andrew Gower, Paul Murray of BT Laboratories; Tom Fuke of SiliconGraphics Computer Systems, Reading, CAD Centre, Cambridge (pp. 48–49); Nicholas C. Thompson, Cole Thompson Associates, Architects, Project Director, INTEGER Intelligent & Green Housing Project (pp. 20–21); Brian Bloor, Ian Holden, and Tony Davison of IBM United Kingdom Limited; Neil Johannessen, curator of the British Telecom Museum, London; Veneta Paul of the Science Museum, London; Rosie Hayes of the Oxford Institute of Virology and Environmental Biology; Nathan Powell of the Meteorological Office; SegaWorld; Gerald Armin; Gary Ombler.

Editorial and research assistance: Katie Martin, Joanne Matthews, and Robert Graham

Design assistance: Catharine Goldsmith

Special photography: Steve Gorton, Dave King

Additional photography: Jane Burton, Andy Crawford, Philip Dowell, Philip Garward, Dave King, Ian O'Leary, Tim Ridley, Jane Stockman, Clive Streeter Illustrators: Joanne Connor, Nicholas Hill

Index: Marion Dent

Picture Credits
The publisher would like to thank the following for their kind permission to reproduce their photographs:

(a = above, b = below, c = center, l = left, r = right, t = top)

AKG, London: Archaeological Museum, Florence 36tr.
Arcaid: Neil Troiano 22-23c.
Associated Press: Technos Japan 33c.
Chas. A. Blatchford & Sons Ltd.: 41bra.
Blaupunkt: 25c.
Bridgeman Art Library, London/New York: Staatliche Museen, Berlin 8bc.
© **British Library Board:** 49cr.
Reproduced with permission of Applied Research and Technology Department, BT Labs: 4tc, tr, 6tl, bl, 28-29, 59tr, br.
'Coca-Cola', 'Coke', and the Dynamic Ribbon device are registered trade marks of The Coca-Cola Company and are reproduced with kind permission from **The Coca-Cola Company:** 17c.
Corbis: Roger Ressmeyer 11tc, 49tr; Michael S. Yamashita 27ca.
Corbis-Bettmann: 8tl, 12tl, 34cl; UPI 48tl, 52cla.
Daimler Benz: 4bl, 26cl, b.
Diners' Club: 10tc.
Energy Research and Generation, Inc.: 55tr.
Ecoscene: John Farhar 12cr.
ESA: 59bl.
Mary Evans Picture Library: 8cb, cra, 22bl, 26tl, 42bl, 45cl, 57br, 59cla; Sigmund Freud Copyrights 32tr.
Future Systems, London: 4c, 19b.
John Frost Newspapers: *Evening Standard* / Solo: Ken Towner 40cr.
Pascal Goetgheluck: 58b.
The Ronald Grant Archive: *The Fifth Element* (1997) Guild 27crb; *1984* (1956) Associated British Pathé 14tr; *Star Trek: Next Generation* (TV) Paramount Television 40b; *2001, A Space Odyssey* (1969) MGM 44tl.
Robert Harding Picture Library: Charlie Westerman 55tc.
Honda (UK): 18cb.
Hulton Getty: 8tr, cr, 9cb, crb, 10tl.
The Hutchison Library: Bernard Régent 16-17b; Liba Taylor 17tl.

The Image Bank: Archive Photos 58c; Scott Sutton 48cl.
Ann Ronan at Image Select: 32tl.
IBM: 11tr, 58cl.
Courtesy of the Kobal Collection: *Robocop* Orion Pictures (1987) 40cr.
Lotus Cars: 54b.
The Met. Office: 15tr.
The Movie Store Collection: *Batman Forever* Warner Bros. (1995) 33tr; *The Time Machine* MGM/Galaxy (1960) 57tl.
NASA: 10cr, 38tl, 50cb, 57tr.
National Motor Museum, Beaulieu: 19tl.
Natural History Photographic Agency: GI Bernard 36-37b; Daniel Heuclin 36cr.
The Robert Opie Collection: 9tc.
Picture courtesy of Panasonic: 53tl.
Pepsi IMAX Theatre: 49tl.
'Vision of the future' images supplied by Philips Electronics: 30cl, bl, c, bc, br, 31, 59tl.
Psion Computers plc.: (screen) 52bc.
Quadrant Picture Library: Flight/Wagner 27cl.
Rex Features: 10clb, 18cr, 24bl, tl, 26cr, 27bl, 42br, 43br, 55cl; Neil Stevenson 11crb; Greg Williams 13c, ca, 41br.
Roslin Institute, Roslin: 37ca.
Science Photo Library: 37br; Julian Baum 38cl, 56cl, 57cr; John Bavosi 34tr; A. Barrington Brown 10cb; J. Bernholc et al., North Carolina State University 5c, 54cl; Dale Boyer 12bl; Jean-Loup Charmet 8bl; Custom Medical Stock Photo 34bc; Earth Satellite Corporation 15tl; ESA/PLI 12-13b; Ken Eward 35tl; Simon Fraser 37cr; Simon Fraser/RVI Newcastle-upon-Tyne 36cb; GE Astro Space 12cr; Guntram Gerst, Peter Arnold Inc. 12br; GJLP-CNRI 33br; Klaus Guldbrandsen 40bra, 49br; Victor Habbick Visions 56-57c; David Hall 18cl; David Hardy 56bl; W. Haxby, Lamont Doherty Earth Observatory 51tr; James Holmes 32-33b; Ducros Jerrican 13bl, 25cl; Mura Jerrican 43bl; James King-Holmes 41tr, 53cb; Mehau Kulyk 34cr, br; Lawrence Livermore National Laboratory 55b; Massonnet et al./CNES 51tl; John Mead 18bl; Peter Menzel 43cl; Hank Morgan 33tc, 44cb, 45tl, 47cl, c; Nelson Morris 52tl; NASA

11cra, 14bl, 27t, tl, 43tl; NASA/Goddard Institute for Space Studies 15cra; /Space Telescope Science Institute 50bl; NCSA/University of Illinois 12cl; NOAA 15tc; David Parker 58cr; Philippe Plailly 32bl; Philippe Plailly/Eurelios 37tr; Catherine Pouedras/MNHN /Eurelios 40c; Rosenfeld Images Ltd. 37cr; Volker Steger, Peter Arnold Inc. 40tl; James Stevenson 41tc; Weiss, Jerrican 13tr; U.S. Department of Energy 42l; Erik Viktor 35cl.
Science Museum, London: 9cr.
Science Museum/Science & Society Picture Library: 4-5b, 6r, 19tc, tr, 22-23t, 41l, 52b, 53c, tr, bc, 54cl, cra, 54-55t.
Shimuzu Corporation, Space Systems Division, Tokyo: 22bl.
Frank Spooner Pictures: Gamma: Nicolas Le Corre 50br, 51bl; Alexis Duclos 16cl; Kaku Kurita 23b, 43tc, tr; Pascal Maitre 17tr; Gamma Liaison: Steven Burr Williams /simulation display courtesy of Massachusetts Institute of Technology/digital composition by Slim Films 25b.
Tony Stone Images: Paul Chesley 22br, 25c; Ross Harrison Koty 51c; Don Lowe 17cl; Andy Sacks 38bl.
Sygma: A. H. Bingen 51br; Hank Morgan 44cb, 45tl; A. Nogues 16tl; Ilkka Uimonen 44cb; I. Wyman 3clb.
Tate Gallery Publications: *The Reckless Sleeper* (1927) Rene Magritte © ADAGP, Paris and DACS, London 1998 32c.
Telegraph Colour Library: 16cr, 22bc, 25tr, 34bl, 58tr; Paul Windsor 55cr.
Vintage Magazine Company: 13tl, 18tl, 24tl, cl, 30tl, 50tl, 56tl, 58tl.
Volvo Car Corporation: 50c, cr.

Jacket: reproduced with permission of **Applied Research and Technology Department, BT Labs:** front cra, bc.
The Movie Store Collection: *The Time Machine* (1960) MGM/Galaxy front bl.
Rex Features: front tr.
Science Photo Library: J. Bernholc et al., North Carolina State University spine; GJLP-CNRI front c; John Mead front cla.
Science Museum/Science & Society Picture Library: front br.

DK EYEWITNESS BOOKS

SUBJECTS

HISTORY

AFRICA

ANCIENT CHINA

ARMS & ARMOR

BATTLE

CASTLE

COWBOY

EXPLORER

KNIGHT

MEDIEVAL LIFE

MYTHOLOGY

NORTH AMERICAN INDIAN

PIRATE

PRESIDENTS

RUSSIA

SHIPWRECK

TITANIC

VIKING

WITCHES & MAGIC-MAKERS

ANCIENT WORLDS

ANCIENT EGYPT

ANCIENT GREECE

ANCIENT ROME

AZTEC, INCA & MAYA

BIBLE LANDS

MUMMY

PYRAMID

THE BEGINNINGS OF LIFE

ARCHEOLOGY

DINOSAUR

EARLY HUMANS

PREHISTORIC LIFE

THE ARTS

BOOK

COSTUME

DANCE

FILM

MUSIC

TECHNOLOGY

BOAT

CAR

FLYING MACHINE

FUTURE

INVENTION

SPACE EXPLORATION

TRAIN

PAINTING

GOYA

IMPRESSIONISM

LEONARDO & HIS TIMES

MANET

MONET

PERSPECTIVE

RENAISSANCE

VAN GOGH

WATERCOLOR

SCIENCE

ASTRONOMY

CHEMISTRY

EARTH

ECOLOGY

ELECTRICITY

ELECTRONICS

ENERGY

EVOLUTION

FORCE & MOTION

HUMAN BODY

LIFE

LIGHT

MATTER

MEDICINE

SKELETON

TECHNOLOGY

TIME & SPACE

SPORT

BASEBALL

FOOTBALL

OLYMPICS

SOCCER

SPORTS

ANIMALS

AMPHIBIAN

BIRD

BUTTERFLY & MOTH

CAT

DOG

EAGLE &
BIRDS OF PREY

ELEPHANT

FISH

GORILLA,
MONKEY & APE

HORSE

INSECT

MAMMAL

REPTILE

SHARK

WHALE

HABITATS

ARCTIC & ANTARCTIC

DESERT

JUNGLE

OCEAN

POND & RIVER

SEASHORE

THE EARTH

CRYSTAL & GEM

FOSSIL

HURRICANE &
TORNADO

PLANT

ROCKS & MINERALS

SHELL

TREE

VOLCANO &
EARTHQUAKE

WEATHER

THE WORLD AROUND US

BUILDING

CRIME & DETECTION

FARM

FLAG

MEDIA &
COMMUNICATIONS

MONEY

RELIGION

SPY

Future updates and editions will be available online at www.dk.com

A–Z

DK EYEWITNESS BOOKS

1–110

Future updates and editions will be available online at www.dk.com